CHINATOWN

Chinatown

Robert Towne

faber and faber

Curly responds slowly, rising to his feet, crying. Gittes reaches into his desk and pulls out a shot glass, quickly selects a cheaper bottle of bourbon from several fifths of more expensive whiskeys.

3 Gittes pours a large shot. He shoves the glass across his desk toward Curly.

GITTES

—Down the hatch.

Curly stares dumbly at it. Then picks it up and drains it. He sinks back into the chair opposite Gittes, begins to cry quietly.

CURLY
(drinking, relaxing a little)
She's just no good.

GITTES

What can I tell you, kid? You're right. When you're right, you're right, and you're right.

CURLY

—Ain't worth thinking about.

Gittes leaves the bottle with Curly.

GITTES

You're absolutely right, I wouldn't give her another thought.

CURLY
(pouring himself)
You know, you're *okay*, Mr. Gittes. I know it's your job, but you're okay.

GITTES
(settling back, breathing a little easier)
Thanks, Curly. Call me Jake.

CURLY

Thanks. You know something, Jake?

GITTES

What's that, Curly?

CURLY

I think I'll kill her.

4 Int. Duffy & Walsh's Office

noticeably less plush than Gittes'. A well-groomed, dark-haired WOMAN sits nervously between their two desks, fiddling with the veil on her pill-box hat.

> WOMAN
> —I was hoping Mr. Gittes could see to this person-
> ally—

> WALSH
> *(almost with the manner of someone comforting the*
> *bereaved)*
> —If you'll allow us to complete our preliminary questioning, by then he'll be free.

There is the SOUND of ANOTHER MOAN coming from Gittes' office—something made of glass shatters. The Woman grows more edgy.

5 Int. Gittes' Office—Gittes & Curly

Gittes and Curly stand in front of the desk, Gittes staring contemptuously at the heavy-breathing hulk towering over him. Gittes takes a handkerchief and wipes away the plunk of perspiration on his desk.

> CURLY
> *(crying)*
> They don't kill a guy for that.

> GITTES
> Oh they don't?

> CURLY
> Not for your wife. That's the unwritten law.

6 Gittes pounds the photos on the desk, shouting:

> GITTES
> I'll tell you the unwritten law, you dumb son of a bitch, you gotta be rich to kill somebody, anybody and get away with it. You think you got that kind of dough, you think you got that kind of class?

Curly shrinks back a little.

> CURLY

...No...

> GITTES

You bet your ass you don't. You can't even pay me
off.

This seems to upset Curly even more.

> CURLY

I'll pay the rest next trip—we only caught sixty ton
of skipjack around San Benedict. We hit a chubasco,
they don't pay you for skipjack the way they do for
tuna or albacore—

> GITTES
> *(easing him out of his office)*

Forget it. I only mention it to illustrate a point. . . .

7 Int. Office Reception

He's now walking him past SOPHIE, who pointedly averts her gaze. He
opens the door where on the pebbled glass can be read: J. J. GITTES AND
ASSOCIATES—DISCREET INVESTIGATION.

> GITTES

I don't want your last dime.

He throws an arm around Curly and flashes a dazzling smile.

> GITTES
> *(continuing)*

What kind of a guy do you think I am?

> CURLY

Thanks, Mr. Gittes.

> GITTES

Call me Jake. Careful driving home, Curly.

He shuts the door on him and the smile disappears.

8 He shakes his head, starting to swear under his breath.

> SOPHIE
> —A Mrs. Mulwray is waiting for you, with Mr.
> Walsh and Mr. Duffy.

Gittes nods, walks on in.

9 Int. Duffy and Walsh's Office

Walsh rises when Gittes enters.

> WALSH
> Mrs. Mulwray, may I present Mr. Gittes?

Gittes walks over to her and again flashes a warm, sympathetic smile.

> GITTES
> How do you do, Mrs. Mulwray?

> MRS. MULWRAY
> Mr. Gittes . . .

> GITTES
> Now, Mrs. Mulwray, what seems to be the prob-
> lem?

She holds her breath. The revelation isn't easy for her.

> MRS. MULWRAY
> My husband, I believe, is seeing another woman.

Gittes looks mildly shocked. He turns for confirmation to his two partners.

> GITTES
> (gravely)
> No, really?

> MRS. MULWRAY
> I'm afraid so.

> GITTES
> I am sorry.

10 Gittes pulls up a chair, sitting next to Mrs. Mulwray—between Duffy and Walsh. Duffy cracks his gum.

Gittes gives him an irritated glance. Duffy stops chewing.

> MRS. MULWRAY
> Can't we talk about this alone, Mr. Gittes?

> GITTES
> I'm afraid not, Mrs. Mulwray. These men are my
> operatives and at some point they're going to assist
> me. I can't do everything myself.

> MRS. MULWRAY
> Of course not.

> GITTES
> Now—what makes you certain he is involved with
> someone?

Mrs. Mulwray hesitates. She seems uncommonly nervous at the question.

> MRS. MULWRAY
> —a wife can tell.

Gittes sighs.

> GITTES
> Mrs. Mulwray, do you love your husband?

> MRS. MULWRAY
> *(shocked)*
> . . . Yes of course.

> GITTES
> *(deliberately)*
> Then go home and forget about it.

> MRS. MULWRAY
> —but . . .

> GITTES
> *(staring intently at her)*
> I'm sure he loves you too. You know the expression
> "Let sleeping dogs lie"? You're better off not
> knowing.

> MRS. MULWRAY
> *(with some real anxiety)*

But I have to know!

Her intensity is genuine. Gittes looks to his two partners.

> GITTES

All right, what's your husband's first name?

> MRS. MULWRAY

Hollis. Hollis Mulwray.

> GITTES
> *(visibly surprised)*

Water and Power?

Mrs. Mulwray nods, almost shyly. Gittes is now casually but carefully checking out the detailing of Mrs. Mulwray's dress—her handbag, shoes, etc.

> MRS. MULWRAY

—he's the Chief Engineer.

> DUFFY
> *(a little eagerly)*

—Chief Engineer?

11 Gittes' glance tells Duffy that Gittes wants to do the questioning. Mrs. Mulwray nods.

> GITTES
> *(confidentially)*

This type of investigation can be hard on your pocketbook, Mrs. Mulwray. It takes time.

> MRS. MULWRAY

Money doesn't matter to me, Mr. Gittes.

Gittes sighs.

> GITTES

Very well. We'll see what we can do.

FARMER drives in several scrawny, bleating sheep. Naturally, they cause a commotion.

> COUNCIL PRESIDENT
> *(shouting to farmer)*
> What in the hell do you think you're doing?
> *(as the sheep bleat down the aisles toward the Council)*
> Get those goddam things out of here!

> FARMER
> *(right back)*
> Tell me where to take them! You don't have an answer for that so quick, do you?

19 Bailiffs and sergeants-at-arms respond to the imprecations of the Council and attempt to capture the sheep and the farmers, having to restrain one who looks like he's going to bodily attack Mulwray.

> FARMER
> *(through above, to Mulwray)*
> —You steal the water from the valley, ruin the grazing, starve my livestock—who's paying you to do that, Mr. Mulwray, that's what I want to know!

20 & 21 Omitted

22 L.A. Riverbed—Long Shot

It's virtually empty. Sun blazes off its ugly concrete banks. Where the banks are earthen, they are parched and choked with weeds.

After a moment Mulwray's car pulls INTO VIEW on a flood-control road about fifteen feet above the riverbed. Mulwray gets out of the car. He looks around.

23 With Gittes

holding a pair of binoculars, downstream and just above the flood-control road—using some dried mustard weeds for cover. He watches while Mulwray makes his way down to the center of the riverbed.

There Mulwray stops, turns slowly, appears to be looking at the bottom of the riverbed, or—at nothing at all.

24 Gittes

trains the binoculars on him. Sun glints off Mulwray's glasses.

25 Below Gittes

There's the SOUND of something like champagne corks popping. Then a small Mexican boy atop a swayback horse rides into the river and into Gittes' view.

26 Mulwray

himself stops, stands still when he hears the sound. Power lines and the sun are overhead, the trickle of brackish water at his feet.

He moves swiftly downstream in the direction of the sound, toward Gittes.

27 Gittes

moves a little farther back as Mulwray rounds the bend in the river and comes face-to-face with the Mexican boy on the muddy banks. Mulwray says something to the boy.

The boy doesn't answer at first. Mulwray points to the ground. The boy gestures. Mulwray frowns. He kneels down in the mud and stares at it. He seems to be concentrating on it.

28 After a moment he rises, thanks the boy, and heads swiftly back upstream—scrambling up the bank to his car.

There he reaches through the window and pulls out a roll of blueprints or something like them—he spreads them on the hood of his car and begins to scribble some notes, looking downstream from time to time.

The power lines overhead HUM.

He stops, listens to them—then rolls up the plans and gets back in the car. He drives off.

29 Gittes

hurries to get back to his car. He gets in and gets right back out. The steamy leather burns him. He takes a towel from the backseat and carefully places it on the front one. He gets in and takes off.

30 Omitted

31 Point Fermin Park—Dusk

Streetlights go on.

32 Mulwray

pulls up, parks. Hurries out of the car, across the park lawn, and into the shade of some trees and buildings.

33 Gittes

pulls up, moves across the park at a different angle, but in the direction Mulwray had gone. He makes it through the trees in time to see Mulwray scramble adroitly down the side of the cliff to the beach below. He seems in a hurry. Gittes moves after him—having a little more difficulty negotiating the climb than Mulwray did.

34 Down on the Beach

Gittes looks to his right—where the bay is a long, clear crescent. He looks to his left—there's a promontory of sorts. It's apparent Mulwray has gone that way. Gittes hesitates, then moves in that direction—but climbs along the promontory in order to be above Mulwray.

35 At the Outfall

Gittes spots Mulwray just below him, kicking at the sand.

Mulwray picks up a starfish. Brushes sand off it. Looks absently up toward Gittes.

36 Gittes

backs away, sits near the outfall, yawns.

37 Beacon Light at Point Fermin

flashing in the dust.

38 Close—Gittes

sitting, suddenly starts. He swears softly—he's in a puddle of water, and the seat of his trousers is wet.

39 Mulwray

below him, is watching the water trickling down from the outfall near Gittes.

Mulwray stands and stares at the water, apparently fascinated. Even as Gittes watches Mulwray watching, the volume and velocity seem to increase until it gushes in spurts, cascading into the sea, whipping it into a foam.

40 At the Street—Gittes' Car

There's a slip of paper stuck under the windshield wiper. Gittes pulls it off, gets in the car, and turns on the dash light. It says: SAVE OUR CITY! LOS ANGELES IS DYING OF THIRST! PROTECT YOUR PROPERTY! LOS ANGELES IS YOUR INVESTMENT IN THE FUTURE!!! VOTE YES NOVEMBER 6. CITIZENS COMMITTEE TO SAVE OUR CITY, HON. SAM BAGBY, FORMER MAYOR—CHAIRMAN. Gittes grumbles, crumples it up, and tosses it out the window. He notices other flyers on a couple of cars down the street.

Gittes reaches down and opens his glove compartment.

41 Int. Glove Compartment

consists of a small mountain of Ingersoll pocket watches.

The cheap price tags are still on them. Gittes pulls out one.

He absently winds it, checks the time with his own watch. It's 9:37 as he walks to Mulwray's car and places it behind the front wheel of Mulwray's car. He yawns again and heads back to his own car.

42 Gittes

arrives whistling, opens the door with J. J. GITTES AND ASSOCIATES—DISCREET INVESTIGATION on it.

GITTES
Morning, Sophie.

Sophie hands him a small pile of messages. He goes through them.

                                 GITTES

Walsh here?

                                 SOPHIE

He's in the darkroom.

43 Gittes walks through his office to Duffy and Walsh's. A little red light is on in the corner, over a closed door. Gittes walks over and knocks on the door.

                                 GITTES

Where'd he go yesterday?

                              WALSH'S VOICE

Three reservoirs—men's room of a Richfield gas station on Flower, and the Pig 'n Whistle.

                                 GITTES

Jesus Christ, this guy's really got water on the brain.

                              WALSH'S VOICE

What'd you expect? That's his job.

                                 GITTES

Listen, we can't string this broad out indefinitely—
we got to come up with something.

                              WALSH'S VOICE

I think I got something.

                                 GITTES

Oh, yeah? You pick up the watch?

44 Int. Duffy & Walsh's Office—Gittes

                              WALSH'S VOICE

It's on your desk. Say, you hear the one about the
guy who goes to the North Pole with Admiral Byrd
looking for penguins?

Gittes walks to his office.

45 On His Desk

is the Ingersoll watch, the crystal broken—the hands stopped at 2:47.

GITTES

He was there all night.

Gittes drops it, sits down. Walsh comes in carrying a series of wet photos stuck with clothespins onto a small blackboard.

GITTES
(continuing, eagerly)

So what you got?

Walsh shows him the photos. He looks at them. They are a series outside a restaurant showing Mulwray with another older man whose appearance is striking. In two of the photos a gnarled cane is visible.

GITTES
(continuing, obviously annoyed)

This?

WALSH

They got into a terrific argument outside the Pig 'n Whistle.

GITTES

What about?

WALSH

I don't know—the traffic was pretty loud. I only heard one thing—apple core.

GITTES

Apple core?

WALSH
(shrugs)

Yeah.

46 Int. Gittes' Office

Gittes tosses down the photos in disgust.

GITTES

Jesus Christ, Walsh—that's what you spent your day doing?

WALSH

Look, you tell me to take pictures, I take pictures.

>   GITTES
>   Let me explain something to you, Walsh—this busi-
>   ness requires a certain finesse—

The PHONE has been RINGING. Sophie buzzes him.

>   GITTES
>   Yeah, Sophie?
>   *(he picks up the phone)*
>   Duffy, where are you?

Duffy's VOICE can be HEARD, excitedly: "I got it. I got it. He's found himself some cute little twist—in a rowboat, in Echo Park."

>   GITTES
>   *(continuing)*
>   Okay, slow down—Echo Park—
>   *(to Walsh)*
>   Jesus, water again.

47 Westlake Park (McArthur Park)

Duffy is rowing, Gittes seated in the stern.

They pass Mulwray, and a slender blonde girl in a summer-print dress, drifting in their rowboat, Mulwray fondly doting on the girl.

>   GITTES
>   *(to Duffy, as they pass)*
>   Let's have a big smile, pal.

He shoots past Duffy, expertly running off a couple of fast shots. Mulwray and the girl seem blissfully unaware of them.

48 Duffy

turns again, and they row past Mulwray and the girl, Gittes again clicking off several fast shots.

49 Close Shot—Sign (El Macando Apartments)

MOVE ALONG the red-tiled roof and down to a lower level of the roof, where Gittes' feet are hooked over the apex of the roof and Gittes himself is stretched face downward on the tiles, pointing himself and his camera to a veranda below him where the girl and Mulwray are eating. Gittes is clicking off more shots when the tiles his feet are hooked over come loose.

Gittes begins a slow slide down the tile to the edge of the roof—and possibly over it to a three-story drop. He tries to slow himself down. The loose tile also begins to slide.

Gittes stops himself at the roof's edge by the storm drain and begins a very precarious turn—this time hooking his feet in the drain itself. The loose tile falls and hits the veranda below. He stops as it's about to slide over the edge. He carefully lays it in the drain. But a fragment of the cracked edge of the tile falls.

50 With Mulwray and the Girl

Mulwray staring at the fragment at his feet. He looks to the girl. He's clearly concerned. He rises, looks up to the roof.

51 From his POV

The roof and the sign topping it betray nothing. He slowly sits back down, staring at the tile fragment.

52 Close Shot—Newspaper

DEPARTMENT OF WATER AND POWER BLOWS FUSE OVER CHIEF'S USE OF FUNDS FOR EL MACANDO LOVE NEST.

In the style of the Hearst yellow press, there is a heart-shaped drawing around one of the photos that Gittes had taken. Next to it is a smaller column, "J.J. Gittes Hired by Suspicious Spouse."

53 Int. Barbershop—Gittes

holds the paper and reads while getting his hair cut and his shoes shined. In fact, almost all the customers are reading papers.

> BARNEY
> *(to Gittes)*
> —when you get so much publicity, after a while you
> must get blasé about it.

A self-satisfied smile comes to Gittes' face.

> BARNEY
> *(continuing)*
> Face it. You're practically a movie star.

In b.g., customers can be OVERHEARD talking about the drought. Interspersed with above, someone is saying, "They're gonna start rationing water unless it rains." Someone else says, "Only for washing your cars." Third says, "You're not going to be able to water your lawn either, or take a bath more than once a week." First says, "If you don't have a lawn or a car, do you get an extra bath?"

54 Gittes has been staring outside the barbershop. A car is stalled. The hood is up. A man watches his radiator boiling over.

> GITTES
> *(laughing)*
> Look at that.

> BARNEY
> Heat's murder.

> OTHER CUSTOMER
> *(end of conversation)*
> "Fools' names and fools' faces . . ."

55 Gittes has heard the word. He straightens up.

> GITTES
> *(smiling to Other Customer)*
> What's that, pal?

> OTHER CUSTOMER
> *(indicating paper)*
> Nothing—you got a hell of a way to make a living.

> GITTES
> —Oh? What do you do to make ends meet?

> OTHER CUSTOMER
> Mortgage Department, First National Bank.

Gittes laughs.

> GITTES
> Tell me, how many people a week do you foreclose
> on?

OTHER CUSTOMER

We don't publish a record in the paper, I can tell you
that.

GITTES

Neither do I.

OTHER CUSTOMER

No, you have a press agent do it.

Gittes gets out of the chair. Barney, a little concerned, tries to restrain him,
holding on to the barber sheet around Gittes' neck.

GITTES

Barney, who is this bimbo? He a regular customer?

BARNEY

Take it easy, Jake.

GITTES

Look, pal—I make an honest living. People don't
come to me unless they're miserable and I help 'em
out of a bad situation. I don't kick them out of their
homes like you jerks who work in the bank.

BARNEY

Jake, for Christ's sake.

56 Gittes is trying to take off his sheet.

GITTES

C'mon, get out of the barber chair. We'll go outside
and talk this over—

The Customer is shrinking back into the chair.

BARNEY

Hey, c'mon, Jake. Sit down. Sit down—you hear
about the fella goes to his friend and says, "What'll I
do, I'm tired of screwing my wife?" And his friend
says, "Whyn't you do what the Chinese do?"

Gittes allows himself to be tugged back to his chair.

>   GITTES
> I don't know how that got in the paper, as a matter
> of fact—it surprised me, it was so quick. I make an
> honest living.

>   BARNEY
> 'Course you do, Jake.

>   GITTES
> An honest living.

>   BARNEY
>   *(continuing)*
> So anyway, he says, 'hyn't you do what the Chinese
> do?'

57 Int. Gittes' Office

Gittes comes bursting in, slapping a newspaper on his thigh.

>   GITTES
> Duffy, Walsh—

Walsh comes out of his office, Duffy out of the other one.

>   GITTES
>   *(continuing)*
> Sophie—go to the little girl's room for a minute.

>   SOPHIE
> But, Mr. Gittes—

>   GITTES
>   *(insisting)*
> Sophie—

>   SOPHIE
> Yes, Mr. Gittes.

She gets up and leaves.

>   GITTES
> —so there's this fella who's tired of screwing his
> wife—

DUFFY

Jake, listen—

GITTES

Shut up, Duffy, you're always in a hurry—and his
friend says why not do what the Chinese do? So he
says, what do they do? His friend says the Chinese
they screw for a while—Just listen a second,
Duffy—

A stunning YOUNG WOMAN appears behind Gittes in his doorway.
She's shortly joined by a small, GRAY-HAIRED MAN. They listen, un-
seen by Gittes.

GITTES
(continuing)

—and then they stop and they read a little Confu-
cius and they screw some more, and they stop and
they smoke some opium and then they go back and
screw some more, and they stop again and they con-
template the moon or something, and it makes it
more exciting. So this other guy goes home to screw
his wife, and after a while he stops and gets up and
goes into the other room, only he reads *Life* maga-
zine and he goes back and he screws some more and
suddenly says excuse me a second and he gets up
and smokes a cigarette and he goes back and by this
time his wife is getting sore as hell. So he screws
some more and then he gets up to look at the moon,
and his wife says, "What the hell do you think
you're doing?
(Gittes breaks up)
. . . you're screwing like a Chinaman."

**58 Gittes hangs on to Sophie's desk, laughing his ass off. The little Gray-
haired Man winces. When Gittes looks up, he sees the Young Woman,
apparently in her late twenties. She's so stunning that Gittes nearly
gasps.**

YOUNG WOMAN

Mr. Gittes?

                                GITTES
        Yes?

                            YOUNG WOMAN
        Do you know me?

                                GITTES
        Well—I think I—I would've remembered.

                            YOUNG WOMAN
        Have we ever met?

                                GITTES
        Well, no.

                            YOUNG WOMAN
        Never?

                                GITTES
        Never.

                            YOUNG WOMAN
        That's what I thought. You see, I'm Mrs. Evelyn
        Mulwray—you know, Mr. Mulwray's wife?

59 Gittes is staggered. He glances down at the newspaper.

                                GITTES
        Not *that* Mulwray?

                                EVELYN
        Yes, that Mulwray, Mr. Gittes. And since you agree
        with that me we've never met, you must also agree
        that I haven't hired you to do anything—certainly
        not spy on my husband. I see you like publicity, Mr.
        Gittes. Well, you're going to get it—

                                GITTES
        Now wait a minute, Mrs. Mulwray . . .

She's walked past him toward the door. He stops her.

GITTES
(continuing)
—there's some misunderstanding here. It's not
going to do any good to get tough with me—

Evelyn flashes a cold smile.

EVELYN
I don't get tough with anybody, Mr. Gittes. My law-
yer does.

Evelyn starts out the door, and Gittes starts after her. This time he's
stopped by the Gray-haired Man, who has also come out of his office and
up behind him.

GRAY-HAIRED MAN
Here's something for you, Mr. Gittes—

Gittes turns to be handed a thick sheaf of papers, a summons and a com-
plaint. Evelyn walks out the door.

GRAY-HAIRED MAN
(continuing pleasantly)
I suppose we'll be hearing from your attorney.

Gittes stares down at the papers in his hand.

60 Int. Gittes' Inner Office—Gittes, Duffy & Walsh

On Gittes' desk there are empty coffee cups, the summons and the com-
plaint, and the newspaper Gittes had brought with him from the barbershop.

The three men are sitting, worn and silent. Walsh chewing gum is the
loudest noise in the room.

Gittes looks to Walsh with obvious irritation. Walsh stops chewing.

Duffy puts out a cigarette in the dregs of one of the coffee cups.

GITTES
(to Duffy)
There's seven ashtrays in this room, Duffy.

DUFFY
Okay.

                          GITTES

That's a filthy habit.

                          DUFFY

I said okay, Jake.

                          GITTES

Yeah, yeah—if she'd come in here saying she was
Shirley Temple you'd say okay to that too.

                          WALSH

Look, Jake—she give us Mulwray's real phone
number and address—

                          GITTES

All she needed for that was the phone book!

                          WALSH

No, no—she said not to call, her husband might answer.

                          GITTES

—when I find out who that phony bitch was—

Gittes is staring down at the newspaper. He suddenly grabs the phone,
begins dialing. A tight little smile breaks out on his face. He buzzes Sophie.

                          GITTES

Sophie.

                          SOPHIE

Yes, Mr. Gittes.

                          GITTES

Get me the Times—Whitey Mehrholtz—
                      (as he waits)
And how about that snotty broad?
                      (the phone to his ear)
What does she think, she's perfect? Coming in wav-
ing her lawyers and her money at me—so goddamn
smug. She's no better than anybody else in this
town—

Sophie BUZZES.

GITTES
(continuing)

Whitey, what's new, pal? . . . Yeah, listen, where
did you get those photographs. . . . Yeah, blowing
a fuse over the El Macando love nest—that's cute,
Whitey . . . So who sent them to you . . . *I* sent them?
(Gittes laughs a little hysterically)

Why would I be asking how you get them if *I* sent
them? . . . Whitey? . . . Whitey? . . . C'mon, level with
me for once, my tit's in the wringer and it's beginning to hurt. . . . Yeah. . . . Yeah—yeah.

He hangs up.

WALSH

So he says *you* sent them?

GITTES
(after a moment)

They're all a bunch of phonies.

61 Omitted

62 Int. Department Water & Power—Hall

Gittes stops outside a door marked: HOLLIS I. MULWRAY, CHIEF ENGINEER.

63 He enters an outer office. The SECRETARY looks surprised.

GITTES

Mr. Mulwray, please.

SECRETARY

He's not in, Mr.—

GITTES

Gittes.

SECRETARY

May I ask what this is regarding?

GITTES

It's personal. Has he been out long?

                              SECRETARY
Since lunch.

                               GITTES
Gee whiz—
                    (he glances at his watch)
—and I'm late.

                              SECRETARY
He was expecting you?

                               GITTES
Fifteen minutes ago. Why don't I go in and wait?

Without waiting for a response, he does. The Secretary half rises in protest, but Gittes is through the inner door.

64 Mulwray's Inner Office

The walls are covered with commendations, photos of Mulwray at various construction sites, large maps of watershed areas and reservoirs in the city. On the desk is a framed, tinted photo of Evelyn in riding clothes.

Gittes moves to the desk, watching the translucent pane in the upper half of the door leading to the outer office as he does.

He begins to open and close the desk drawers after quickly examining the top. He tries one of the drawers and it doesn't open. He reopens the top drawer, and the bottom one opens.

He looks in it, pulls out a checkbook. He opens it—riffles through the stubs like he was shuffling cards. Drops it—finds a set of keys, an old phone book, and a menu from a Water Department lunch at the Biltmore Hotel in 1913. Then Gittes hauls out the blueprints that Mulwray had laid across the hood of his car—they read in bold type: WATERSHED AND DRAINAGE SYSTEM FOR THE LOS ANGELES BASIN.

He flips through them—reads one notation in Mulwray's neat hand: "Tues. night. Oak Pass Res.—7 channels used."

Gittes spots a shadow looming in front of the translucent pane. He quickly tosses item after item back, kneeing the drawer—nearly knocking a spare pair of Mulwray's glasses off the desktop when he does. He catches them, puts them on the desk, and is pacing the room as the door opens.

65 Russ Yelburton

enters the room. An anxious Secretary is right behind him.

> YELBURTON
>
> Can I help you?
> *(extending his hand)*
> Russ Yelburton, Deputy Chief in the Department.

> GITTES
> *(equally pleasant)*
> J. J. Gittes—and it's not a departmental matter.

> YELBURTON
> I wonder if you'd care to wait in my office?

This is more a request than an invitation. Gittes nods, follows Yelburton out through the outer office to his offices down the hall.

> YELBURTON
> *(continuing as they're going)*
> You see—this whole business in the paper with Mr.
> Mulwray has us all on edge—

66 Int. Yelburton Office

Smaller than Mulwray's, he has most noticeably a lacquered marlin mounted on the wall. There are a couple of other pictures of Yelburton with yellowtail and other fish he's standing beside.

There's also a small burgee of a fish with the initials A. C. below it, tacked onto the wall.

> YELBURTON
> After all, you work with a man for a certain length
> of time, you come to know him, his habits, his val-
> ues, and so forth—well, either he's the kind who
> chases after women or he isn't.

> GITTES
> And Mulwray isn't?

> YELBURTON
> He never even kids about it.

> GITTES
> Maybe he takes it very seriously.

67 Gittes winks. Yelburton chuckles appreciatively, loosening up a little.

> GITTES
>
> You don't happen to know where Mr. Mulwray's
> having lunch?

> YELBURTON
>
> I'm sorry, I—

> GITTES
>
> Well, tell him I'll be back.

Gittes spots a card tray on Yelburton's desk.

> GITTES
> *(continuing)*
>
> —Mind if I take one of your cards? In case I want to
> get in touch with you again.

> YELBURTON
>
> Help yourself.

68 Gittes fishes a couple off the tray, puts them in his handkerchief pocket. He goes out the door, nearly running into a man who is standing by the Secretary's desk—about Gittes' age, only a head taller and a foot wider, dressed in a plain suit that fits him about as well as a brown paper bag.

> GITTES
>
> Mulvihill, what are you doing here?

69 Outer Office—Yelburton, Mulvihill, and Gittes

Mulvihill stares at Gittes with unblinking eyes, remains by the desk.

> MULVIHILL
>
> They shut my water off, what's it to you?

> GITTES
>
> How'd you find out? You don't drink it, you don't
> take a bath in it, maybe they sent you a letter. Ah,
> but then you'd have to be able to read.

Mulvihill moves toward Gittes, shaking with fury. Yelburton steps between them.

GITTES
(continuing)
Relax, Mulvihill, glad to see you.
(to Yelburton)
Do you know Claude Mulvihill here?

YELBURTON
Hope so. He's working for us.

GITTES
Doing what?

Yelburton glances uneasily at Mulvihill.

YELBURTON
Frankly, there's been some threats to blow up the
city reservoirs.

GITTES
Any particular reason?

YELBURTON
—It's this darn drought. We've had to ration water
in the valley—farmers are desperate—what can we
do? The rest of the city needs drinking water.

GITTES
Well, you're in luck, Mr. Yelburton.

YELBURTON
How's that?

GITTES
When Mulvihill here was Ventura County sheriff,
rumrunners landed tons of booze in Malibu and
never lost a drop. He ought to be able to hold on to
your water for you.

70 Omitted

71 Gittes

turns off onto a winding road. It goes up into the foothills.

Gittes swerves, missing a dog stretched out lazily in the road. Gittes honks
and yells indignantly at the sleepy animal.

72 Gittes stops on a curve. Above a steep bank and partially hidden is the Mulwray home—designed and constructed with shade and curves that are dramatic. When he turns off the ignition, the distant SOUND of the SURF can be HEARD.

Gittes heads up to the entrance.

73 Ext. Mulwray Home—Gittes

rings the bell. He waits.

A powerful CHINESE BUTLER with heavy hair and a half jacket of gold on one front tooth answers the door.

>   GITTES
>   J. J. Gittes to see Mr. Mulwray.

He hands the Chinese Butler a card from his wallet. The Butler takes it and disappears, leaving Gittes standing in the doorway.

Gittes stands and sweats, watching a Japanese GARDENER trim a hedge. There's a SQUEAKING SOUND. Gittes moves a few feet off the porch.

74 POV—Garage

A chauffeur is washing down a cream-colored Packard with a chamois. Steam rises off the hood. The squeaking has obviously come from the chamois.

75 Chinese Butler

in doorway.

>   CHINESE BUTLER
>   Please.

Gittes looks behind him. The Chinese Butler is gesturing for him to follow.

76 Through the House—Gittes

follows him, trying to check out the rooms as he goes. A maid is cleaning in the den. They pass through it, out some French doors, and along a trellised walkway to a large pond with running water.

>   CHINESE BUTLER
>   You wait, please.

77 Gittes is left standing by the pond. It's suddenly very quiet except for the running water. The pond is overflowing. After a moment the Gardener comes running back. He smiles at Gittes, probes into the pond.

There's something gleaming in the bottom of it. Gittes notes it. After a moment the Gardener drops the long probe—the waters recede.

78 Ext. Pond—Gittes and Japanese Gardener—Day

> GARDENER
> *(to Gittes)*

Bad for glass.

> GITTES
> *(not understanding)*
> Yeah sure. Bad for glass.

The Gardener nods and is off, leaving Gittes staring at the object in the bottom of the pond that is gleaming.

He looks at the tool the Gardener was using, hesitates, picks it up, and starts to probe into the pond himself, toward the gleaming object.

He then spots Evelyn rounding a turn, coming down the trellised pathway. He casually hefts the probe, holds on to it for poise.

Evelyn is wearing jeans that are lathered white on the inside of the thighs and laced with brown horsehair.

She's wearing riding boots, is perspiring a little, but looks younger than she did in the office.

> EVELYN

Yes, Mr. Gittes?

Gittes is a little taken aback at seeing Evelyn. He is annoyed as well. Nevertheless, he is elaborately polite.

> GITTES
> Actually, I'm here to see your husband, Mrs. Mulwray.

He laughs a little nervously. He waits for a reply. There is none. The Chinese Butler appears on the veranda.

                    EVELYN
Would you like something to drink?

                    GITTES
What are you having?

                    EVELYN
Iced tea.

                    GITTES
Yeah—fine, thank you.

Chinese Butler nods, disappears.

79 Ext. Pond and Garden—Mulwray Home—Day

Evelyn sits at a glass-topped table. Gittes joins her.

                    EVELYN
My husband's at the office.

                    GITTES
Actually he's not. And he's moved from his apartment at the *El Macando.*

                    EVELYN
                    (sharply)
That's not *his* apartment.

                    GITTES
Anyway, I—the point is, Mrs. Mulwray, I'm not in business to be loved, but I am in business, and believe me, whoever set up your husband, set me up. L.A.'s a small town, people talk—

He waits for a response. Then:

                    GITTES
                    (continuing uneasily)
I'm just trying to make a living, and I don't want to become a local joke—

                    EVELYN
Mr. Gittes, you've talked me into it. I'll drop the lawsuit.

GITTES

What?

EVELYN

I said I'll drop it.

The iced tea comes on a tray, which Ramon sets down between them.

EVELYN
(continuing pleasantly)
—so let's just—drop the whole thing. Sugar?
Lemon—or both?

GITTES

Mrs. Mulwray?

EVELYN
(as she's mixing one of the drinks)
—Yes, Mr. Gittes?

GITTES

I don't want to drop it.

80 Evelyn looks up. Gittes smiles a little sheepishly.

GITTES

I should talk this over with your husband.

EVELYN
(a little concerned)
. . . Why? . . . What on earth for? Look, Hollis seems
to think you're an innocent man.

GITTES

Well, I been accused of many things, Mrs. Mulwray,
but never that.

Again he laughs a little nervously. Again no reaction.

GITTES
(continuing)
You see, somebody went to a lot of trouble here, and
I want to find out, lawsuit or no lawsuit. *I'm* not the
one who's supposed to be caught with my pants
down . . . so I'd like to see your husband—unless
that's a problem.

EVELYN
(with a slight edge)
What do you mean?

GITTES
May I speak frankly, Mrs. Mulwray?

EVELYN
You may if you can, Mr. Gittes.

GITTES
(determined to be polite)
Well, that little girlfriend, she was attractive—in a cheap sort of way, of course—she's disappeared. Maybe they disappeared together somewhere.

EVELYN
(with rising anger)
Suppose they did. How does it concern you?

GITTES
—Nothing personal, Mrs. Mulwray. I just—

EVELYN
It's very personal. It couldn't be more personal. Is this a business or an obsession with you?

GITTES
Look at it this way. Now this phony broad—excuse the language—says she's you, she's hired me. Whoever put her up to it didn't have anything against me. They were out to get your husband. Now, if I see him, I can help him. . . . did you talk this morning?

81 Evelyn brushes lightly at the horsehair on her jeans.

EVELYN
—No. I went riding rather early—

GITTES
—Looks like you went quite a distance—

> EVELYN

No, just riding bareback, that's all. Anyway, you might try the Oak Pass or Stone Canyon Reservoirs—sometimes at lunch Hollis takes walks around them—otherwise he'll be home by 6:30.

> GITTES

I'll stop by.

> EVELYN

Please call first.

Gittes nods.

82 Ext. Oak Pass Reservoir—Day

Gittes drives up a winding road, following a flood channel up into the parched hills.

83 Two Fire Trucks

one a rescue truck, are at the entrance to the reservoir.

The chain-link fence with its KEEP OUT sign is open, and there are people milling around. The reservoir is below.

Gittes' car is stopped by a couple of UNIFORMED POLICE.

> GUARD

Sorry, this is closed to the public, sir.

Gittes hesitates only a moment, then:

> GITTES
> *(to the Guard)*

It's all right—Russ Yelburton, Deputy Chief in the Department.

He fishes out one of Yelburton's cards from his handkerchief pocket—hands it to the Guard.

> GUARD

Sorry, Mr. Yelburton. Go on down.

84 Gittes drives past the Guards, through the gate, along the reservoir. He spots a police car and an unmarked one as well.

Gittes stops and gets out of the car. Several men with their backs turned, one talking quietly, are staring down into the reservoir where other men in small skiffs are apparently dredging for something.

One of the men turns and sees Gittes. He recognizes Gittes and is visibly shocked.

> LOACH
>
> Gittes—for chrissakes—

> GITTES
>
> Loach—

> LOACH
> *(moving to Gittes, taking him by the arm)*
> C'mon, get out of here before—

85 Ext. Reservoir—Day

Loach tries to ease him down the path.

> GITTES
>
> Before what? What the hell's going on?

At the sound of his raised voice, a man standing at the edge of the channel, talking to two boys in swimming trunks, turns around. He's a tall, sleek Mexican in his early thirties, LUIS ESCOBAR.

Both Gittes and Escobar register considerable surprise at seeing one another. The men around them are extremely uneasy.

Loach is actually sweating. Finally, Escobar smiles.

> ESCOBAR
>
> Hello, Jake.

> GITTES
> *(without smiling)*
> How are you, Lou?

> ESCOBAR
>
> —I have a cold I can't seem to shake, but other than that, I'm fine.

GITTES

Summer colds are the worst.

ESCOBAR

Yeah, they are.

Gittes reaches into his pocket, pulls out his cigarette case.

A FIREMAN

No smoking, sir—it's a fire hazard this time of
year—

ESCOBAR

I think we can make an exception—I'll see he's careful with the matches.

GITTES
(lighting up)

Thanks, Lou.

ESCOBAR

How'd you get past the guards?

GITTES

Well, to tell you the truth, I lied a little.

**86 Escobar nods. They walk a couple of steps. The other police—two
plainclothesmen and a uniformed officer—watch them.**

ESCOBAR

You've done well by yourself.

GITTES

I get by.

ESCOBAR

Well, sometimes it takes a while for a man to find
himself and I guess you have.

LOACH

Poking around in other people's dirty linen.

GITTES

Yeah. Tell me. You still throw Chinamen into jail for
spitting on the laundry?

ESCOBAR

You're behind the times, Jake. They've got steam
irons now.

(smiles)

And I'm out of Chinatown.

GITTES

Since when?

ESCOBAR

Since I made lieutenant—

It's apparent Gittes is impressed despite himself.

GITTES

Congratulations.

ESCOBAR

Uh-huh—so what are you doing here?

GITTES

Looking for someone.

ESCOBAR

Who?

GITTES

Hollis Mulwray. You seen him?

ESCOBAR

Oh, yes.

GITTES

I'd like to talk to him.

ESCOBAR

You're welcome to try. There he is.

**87 Escobar points down to the reservoir—a couple of men using poles
with hooks are fishing about in the water. It can be SEEN that one of them
has hooked something.**

He shouts. The other man hooks it too. They pull, revealing the soaking
back of a man's coat—they start to pull the body into the skiff.

88 Int. Coroner's Office—Evelyn and Escobar

are standing over the body of Mulwray. Escobar has the sheet drawn back. Evelyn nods.

Escobar drops the sheet. Escobar and Evelyn move a few feet to one side and whisper, almost as though they were trying to keep the corpse from hearing them.

> ESCOBAR
> —It looks like he was washed the entire length of the runoff channel—could he swim?

> EVELYN
> Of course.

> ESCOBAR
> —Obviously the fall must have knocked him out—

Evelyn nods slightly. Escobar coughs. A coroner's assistant wheels the body out of the office.

> ESCOBAR
> *(continuing)*
> —This alleged affair he was having—the publicity didn't make him morose or unhappy?

89 Outside the Coroner's

Gittes has been sitting on a wooden bench, smoking and listening. At this question he rises and looks through the doorway.

90 Escobar sees him, ignores him. Evelyn doesn't see him.

> EVELYN
> Well, it didn't make him happy . . .

> ESCOBAR
> But there is no possibility he would have taken his own life?

> EVELYN
> *(sharply)*

No.

ESCOBAR
(a little uncomfortably now)
Mrs. Mulwray, do you happen to know the name of
the young woman in question?

Evelyn shows a flash of annoyance.

EVELYN
. . . No.

ESCOBAR
Do you know where she might be?

EVELYN
Certainly not!

Escobar and Evelyn move slowly toward the door.

ESCOBAR
You and your husband never discussed her?

EVELYN
(stopping, faltering)
He . . . we did . . . he wouldn't tell me her name. We
quarreled over her . . . of course—it came as a complete surprise to me—

ESCOBAR
A complete surprise?

EVELYN
—Yes.

ESCOBAR
But I thought you'd hired a private investigator—

EVELYN
. . . A private investigator?

ESCOBAR
(gesturing vaguely toward the door)
Mr. Gittes.

EVELYN
. . . Well, yes—

91 Evelyn looks up to see Gittes standing in the doorway only a foot or two from her. She stops cold. They look at one another for a long moment.

> EVELYN
> *(her eyes on Gittes)*
> . . . But I . . . I . . . did that because I thought it was a
> nasty rumor I'd put an end to. . . .

She finishes, looks plaintively at Gittes. Escobar is right at her back. Gittes says nothing.

> ESCOBAR
> —And when did Mr. Gittes inform you that these
> rumors had some foundation in fact?

Evelyn looks at Escobar but doesn't know how to answer him.

> GITTES
> *(smoothly)*
> —Just before the story broke in the papers, Lou.

92 Escobar nods. They begin to walk slowly, again have to move out of the way as some other corpse is being wheeled out of one of the coroner cubicles.

> ESCOBAR
> —You wouldn't happen to know the present where-
> abouts of the young woman.

> GITTES
> —No.

> ESCOBAR
> Or her name?

> GITTES
> —No.

They have walked a few steps farther down the hall.

> EVELYN
> Will you need me for anything else, Lieutenant?

> ESCOBAR
>
> I don't think so, Mrs. Mulwray. Of course, you have
> my deepest sympathy—and if we need any more in-
> formation, we'll be in touch.

> GITTES
>
> I'll walk her to her car, be right back.

93 Escobar's POV

Evelyn glances at Gittes. They go through a couple of outer doors and
pass several reporters who have been in the outer hall, laughing, kidding,
the tag end of lines like "only in L.A." and "Southern Cafeteria."

Gittes hurries her past the reporters who flank them, asking questions.
Gittes brushes them aside.

94 Evelyn and Gittes—At her car

in a small parking lot.

Evelyn fumbles in her bag, looking feverishly for something in her purse.

> GITTES
>
> Mrs. Mulwray? . . . Mrs. Mulwray.

> EVELYN
> *. . . (flushed, perspiring)*
> . . . Just a minute . . .

> GITTES
> *(touching her gently)*
> —You left your keys in the ignition.

> EVELYN
>
> Oh . . . thank you.

She glances down, leans against the side of the car.

> EVELYN
> *(continuing)*
> . . . Thank you for going along with me. I just didn't
> want to explain anything. . . . I'll send you a check.

> GITTES
> *(puzzled)*

A check?

Evelyn gets in her car.

> EVELYN
> To make it official, I hired you.

She drives off, leaving Gittes gaping.

95 Int. Coroner's Office Hallway

> GITTES
> Don't give me that, Lou. You hauled me down here
> for a statement.

Escobar shrugs.

> ESCOBAR
> I don't want it anymore.

> GITTES
> No?

> ESCOBAR
> No—it was an accident.

> GITTES
> You mean that's what you're going to call it.

Escobar looks up.

> ESCOBAR
> That's right.
> *(contemptuously)*
> Out of respect for his civic position.

Escobar resumes walking.

Gittes laughs.

> GITTES
> What'd he do, Lou, make a pass at your sister?

Escobar stops.

ESCOBAR

No—he drowned a cousin of mine with about five
hundred other people. But they weren't very impor-
tant, just a bunch of dumb Mexicans living by a
dam. Now beat it, Gittes, you don't come out of this
smelling like a rose, you know.

GITTES

Oh, yeah? Can you think of something to charge me
with?

ESCOBAR

When I do, you'll hear about it.

Gittes nods, turns, and walks down the hall.

96 Outside Morgue

Gittes stops by a body on the table, the toe tagged with Mulwray's name.
MORTY is standing near it in a doorway to an adjoining room. A RADIO
is on, and with it the announcement that they're about to hear another
chapter in the life of Lorenzo Jones and his devoted wife, Belle. Another
coroner's assistant sits at the table, listening to the radio and eating a sandwich.

97 Gittes ambles into the room.

MORTY
(a cigarette dangling out of his mouth)
Jake, what're you doin' here?

GITTES

Nothin', Morty, it's my lunch hour. I thought I'd
drop by and see who died lately.

Gittes picks up the sheet and pulls it back. CAMERA GETS ITS FIRST
GLIMPSE of Mulwray's body—eyes open, the face badly cut and bruised.

MORTY

Yeah? Ain't that something? Middle of a drought,
the water commissioner drowns—only in L.A.

GITTES
(looking at Mulwray)
—Yeah—banged up pretty bad—

MORTY

—That's a long fall—

GITTES

—So how are you, Morty?

Morty is wheeling in another body with the help of an assistant.

MORTY

—Never better. You know me, Jake.

As he begins to move the body into the refrigerator, he breaks into a wrenching spasm of coughing. Gittes spots the other body, lowers the sheet on Mulwray.

GITTES
(picking up on cough)
—Yeah—so who you got there?

Morty pulls back the sheet.

MORTY

Leroy Shuhardt, local drunk—used to hang around Ferguson's Alley—

Morty brushes some sand from the man's face, laughs.

MORTY
(continuing)
—Quite a character. Lately he'd been living in one of the downtown storm drains—had a bureau dresser down there and everything.

98 Gittes has already lost interest. He starts away.

GITTES

—Yeah.

MORTY

Drowned too.

This stops Gittes.

GITTES

Come again?

> MORTY

Yeah, got dead drunk, passed out in the bottom of the riverbed.

> GITTES

The L.A. River?

> MORTY
> *(a little puzzled)*

Yeah, under Hollenbeck Bridge, what's wrong with that?

Gittes has moved back to the body, looks at it more closely.

> GITTES

It's bone-dry, Morty.

> MORTY

It's not completely dry.

> GITTES

Yeah, well, he ain't gonna drown in a damp river-bed, either. I don't care how soused he was. That's like drowning in a teaspoon.

Morty shrugs.

> MORTY

We got water out of him, Jake. He drowned.

Gittes walks away mumbling.

> GITTES

Jesus, this town . . .

99 Ext. Sunset Bouievard—Gittes—Day

He's parked on an overpass—the sign HOLLENBECK BRIDGE on one of its concrete columns. Gittes looks down into the riverbed below.

100 From the Bridge

Gittes can see the muddy remains of a collapsed shack, its contents strewn downriver from the bridge. Below him, lying half over the storm drain and one wall that was on the bank of the river is a sign that proclaims OWN YOUR OWN OFFICE IN THIS BUILDING $5000 TO $6000, which was used as a

roof of sorts. Downstream there's the dresser, an oil drum, a Ford seat
cushion, an Armour lard can, etc.—the trashy remains of Shuhardt's
home.

**101 Gittes scrambles down the embankment, and as he lands near the
storm drain, one shoe sinks ankle-deep into mud. Gittes pulls it out,
swearing.**

He begins to walk a little farther downstream when he hears the vaguely
familiar SQUISHY CLOP of something.

Clearing the bridge on the opposite side is the little Mexican Boy, again on
his swayback horse, riding along the muddy bank.

They look at one another a moment.

> GITTES
> *(calling out to him)*
> You were riding here the other day, weren't you?

The Boy doesn't answer.

> GITTES
> *(continuing)*
> Speak English? Habla Ingles?

> THE BOY
> *(finally)*

Si.

> GITTES
> Didn't you talk to a man here—few days ago . . .
> wore glasses . . . he . . .

The Boy nods.

> GITTES
> *(continuing)*
> What did you talk about, mind my asking?

The shadows of the two are very long now.

> THE BOY
> *(finally)*

The water.

> GITTES

What about the water?

> THE BOY

—when it comes.

> GITTES

—When it comes? What'd you tell him?

> THE BOY

Comes in different parts of the river—every night a
different part.

Gittes nods. The horse snorts. The Boy rides slowly on.

102 Ext. Riverbed—Dusk

Gittes scrambles up the embankment to note the direction the storm drain
by Hollenbeck Bridge takes. It is headed above toward the Hollywood
Hills, where the sun is setting.

103 Ext. Gittes in Car—Nightfall

winding his way up a section of the Hollywood Hills. He picks up on an
open flood channel with the spotlight by the driver's windwing.

104 Gittes in Car—Moving

along the flood channel. It is dark now, and Gittes follows the channel
with the car spotlight. He turns at a fork in the road that allows him to
continue following the flood channel.

105 Farther Up—Moving

The road is narrower. Gittes drives more slowly. Foliage is overgrown in
the channel, so its bottom cannot be glimpsed.

106 Still Farther—Night

The road is dirt. Heavy clusters of oak trees and eucalyptus are every-
where. It is very still. Another turn and a pie-shaped view of a lake of
lights in the city below can be GLIMPSED.

107 POV—Chain-link Fence

over the road, bolted. It reads, OAK PASS RESERVOIR. KEEP OUT. NO TRES-
PASSING.

The chain-link itself actually extends over the flood channel and down
into it, making access along the channel itself impossible.

**108 Gittes backs up, turns off the motor, the car lights, the spotlight. A
lone light overhead on tension wires is the sole illumination. There is only
the eerie SOUND of the tension WIRES HUMMING.**

Gittes gets out of the car, climbs the fence near the flood channel itself.

109 On the Other Side

Gittes carefully works his way up through the thick foliage toward a second and larger chain-link fence. Lights from the reservoir still higher
above can be SEEN.

Suddenly there is a GUNSHOT. Then ANOTHER. Gittes dives into the
flood-control channel, which is at this point about four feet deep and six
feet wide. There is the SOUND of men scurrying through the brush, coming near him, then retreating. Gittes loses himself among the ivy in the
channel.

He waits. The men seem to have passed him by. But there is another
SOUND now—an echoing, growing sound. It puzzles Gittes. He starts to
lift his head to catch the direction.

110 Gittes in Flood-Control Channel—Night

Then he's inundated with a rush of water that pours over him, knocks off
his hat, carries him down the channel, banging into its banks, as he des-
perately tries to grab some of the overgrowth to hang on and pull himself
out. But the force of the stream batters him and carries him with it until
he's brought rudely to the chain-link fence. It stops him cold. He's nearly
strained through it.

Swearing and choking, he pulls himself out of the rushing water by means
of the fence itself.

Drenched, battered, he slowly climbs back over the fence and makes his
way toward his car.

111 At Gittes' Car

He fishes for his car keys, looks down—one shoe is missing.

> GITTES
> *(grumbling)*
> Goddam Florsheim shoe, goddammit.

He starts to get into his car, but Mulvihill and a SMALLER MAN stop him—Mulvihill pulling his coat down and pinning his arms—holding him tightly. The smaller man thrusts a switchblade knife about an inch and a half up Gittes' left nostril.

> SMALLER MAN
> *(shaking with emotion)*
> Hold it there, kitty cat.

112 Close—Gittes

frozen, the knife in his nostril, the street lamp overhead gleaming on the silvery blade.

> THE SMALLER MAN
> You are a very nosy fellow, kitty cat. . . . you know
> what happens to nosy fellows?

The Smaller Man actually seems to be trembling with rage when he says this. Gittes doesn't move.

> SMALLER MAN
> *(continuing)*
> Wanna guess? No? Okay. They lose their noses.

With a quick flick the Smaller Man pulls back on the blade, laying Gittes' left nostril open about an inch farther.

Gittes screams. Blood gushes down onto his shirt and coat.

Gittes bends over, instinctively trying to keep the blood from getting on his clothes. Mulvihill and the Smaller Man stare at him.

> THE SMALLER MAN
> *(continuing)*
> Next time you lose the whole thing, kitty cat. I'll cut
> it off and feed it to my goldfish, understand?

MULVIHILL
Tell him you understand, Gittes.

113 Ext. Oak Pass Reservoir—Night

Gittes is now groveling on his hands and knees.

GITTES
(mumbling)
. . . I understand . . .

Gittes, on the ground, can see only his tormentor's two-tone brown-and-white wing-tip shoes—lightly freckled with his blood.

114 The Shoe

comes up and lightly shoves Gittes into the ground. Then the SOUND of FOOTSTEPS RETREATING, Gittes gasping.

115 Int. Gittes' Office—Gittes

sits behind his desk, BACK TO CAMERA, not moving. Duffy sits staring at nothing; Walsh moves uneasily around the room.

The PHONE is RINGING. Sophie BUZZES.

GITTES
(pressing down intercom)
Yeah, Sophie.

SOPHIE'S VOICE
A Miss Sessions calling.

GITTES
Who?

SOPHIE
Ida Sessions.

GITTES
Don't know her—take a number.

116 New Angle—Revealing

a bandage spread-eagle across Gittes' nose.

                              WALSH

So some contractor wants to build a dam and he
makes a few payoffs. So what?

Gittes turns slowly to Walsh. He lightly taps his nose.

                              WALSH
                           (continuing)
Think you can nail Mulvihill? They'll claim you
were trespassing.

                              GITTES

I don't want Mulvihill. I want the big boys that are
making the payoffs.

                              DUFFY

Then what'll you do?

                              GITTES

Sue the shit out of 'em.

                              WALSH

Yeah?

                              GITTES

Yeah—what's wrong with you guys? Think ahead.
We find 'em, sue 'em—we'll make a killing.
                         (a dazzling smile)
We'll have dinner at Chasen's twice a week, we'll be
pissing on ice the rest of our lives.

                              WALSH

Sue people like that, they're liable to be having dinner with the judge who's trying the suit.

Gittes looks irritated. The PHONE RINGS again.

                         SOPHIE'S VOICE

Miss Ida Sessions again. She says you know her.

                              GITTES

Okay.

117 Gittes picks up the phone. He winks to his boys.

> GITTES
>
> Hello, Miss Sessions. I don't believe we've had the pleasure.

> IDA'S VOICE
>
> —oh yes we have . . . are you alone, Mr. Gittes?

> GITTES
> *(clowning a little for the boys)*
> Isn't everybody? What can I do for you, Miss Sessions?

Walsh promptly starts to tell Duffy the Admiral Byrd story.

> IDA'S VOICE
>
> Well, I'm a working girl, Mr. Gittes—I didn't come in to see you on my own.

> GITTES
>
> —When did you come in?

> IDA'S VOICE
>
> —I was the one who pretended to be Mrs. Mulwray, remember?

118 Walsh has finished off the punch line, and both men are laughing raucously. Gittes drops the mail he's been leafing through and puts his hand over the receiver.

> GITTES
> *(to Duffy and Walsh)*
> Shut the fuck up!
> *(then back to Ida)*
> . . . Yes, I remember—nothing, Miss Sessions, just going over a detail or two with my associates. . . . you were saying?

> IDA'S VOICE
>
> . . . Well I never expected anything to happen like what happened to Mr. Mulwray, the point is, if it ever comes out, I want *somebody* to know I didn't know what would happen.

GITTES

—I understand . . . if you could tell me who em-
ployed you, Miss Sessions—that could help us
both—

IDA'S VOICE

Oh no—

GITTES

. . . Why don't you give me your address and we can
talk this over?

IDA'S VOICE

No, Mr. Gittes—just look in the obituary column of
today's Times . . .

GITTES

The obituary column?

IDA'S VOICE

You'll find one of those people—

GITTES

'Those people?' Miss Sessions—

She hangs up. Gittes looks to his two men.

119 Omitted

120 Int. Brown Derby—Close on Newspaper

Gittes is seated, flips through the paper until he finds the OBITUARY
COLUMN, scans it, looks up, abruptly tears the column from the paper
and puts it in his pocket.

When he closes the paper, we can SEE headlines in the left-hand column:
WATER BOND ISSUE PASSES COUNCIL. "Ten-million-dollar referendum to go
before the public."

Evelyn Mulwray is standing at the table as he does so. He rises, allows her
to sit.

121 Close on Evelyn

Gittes watches her as she removes her gloves slowly. She's wearing dove-
gray gabardine—subdued, tailored.

GITTES

Thanks for coming . . . drink?

The waiter's appeared. Evelyn is looking at Gittes' nose.

EVELYN

Tom Collins—with lime, not lemon, please.

Evelyn looks down and smooths her gloves. When she looks back up, she stares expectantly at Gittes.

Gittes pulls out a torn envelope. The initials ECM can be SEEN in a delicate scroll on the corner of it.

GITTES

I got your check in the mail.

EVELYN

Yes. As I said, I was very grateful.

Gittes fingers the envelope. He coughs.

GITTES

Mrs. Mulwray, I'm afraid that's not good enough.

EVELYN
(a little embarrassed)
Well, how much would you like?

GITTES

Stop it. The money's fine. It's generous, but you've shortchanged me on the story.

EVELYN
(coolly)

I have?

GITTES

I think so. Something besides your husband's death was bothering you. You were upset but not that upset.

EVELYN

Mr. Gittes . . .
(icily)
Don't tell me how I feel.

The drinks come. The waiter sets them down.

                          GITTES
Sorry. Look, you sue me, your husband dies, you
drop the lawsuit like a hot potato, and all of it
quicker than wind from a duck's ass—excuse me.
Then you ask me to lie to the police.

                          EVELYN
It wasn't much of a lie.

                          GITTES
—If your husband was killed it was.
                     (meaning check)
—This can look like you paid me off to withhold ev-
idence.

                          EVELYN
But he wasn't killed.

Gittes smiles.

                          GITTES
I think you're hiding something, Mrs. Mulwray.

122 Evelyn remains unperturbed.

                          EVELYN
—Well, I suppose I am . . . actually I knew about the
affair.

                          GITTES
How did you find out?

                          EVELYN
My husband.

                          GITTES
He told you?

Evelyn nods.

                          GITTES
                     (continuing)
—And you weren't the slightest bit upset about it?

                              EVELYN
—I was grateful.

Evelyn, for the first time, appears a little embarrassed.

                              GITTES
        You'll have to explain that, Mrs. Mulwray.

                              EVELYN
—Why?

                              GITTES
                       (a flash of annoyance)
        Look, I do matrimonial work, it's my métier. When
        a wife tells me she's happy her husband is cheating
        on her it runs contrary to my experience.

Gittes looks significantly to Evelyn.

                              EVELYN
        Unless what?

                              GITTES
                      (looking directly at her)
        She's cheating on him.

Evelyn doesn't reply.

                              GITTES
                          (continuing)
—Were you?

123 Evelyn is clearly angry, but she is controlling it.

                              EVELYN
        I don't like the word *cheat*.

                              GITTES
        Did you have affairs?

                              EVELYN
                          (flashing)
        Mr. Gittes—

                              GITTES
        Did he know?

EVELYN
(almost an outburst)
Well, I wouldn't run home and tell him whenever I
went to bed with someone, if that's what you mean.

This subdues Gittes a little. Evelyn is still a little heated.

EVELYN
(continuing more calmly)
—Is there anything else you want to know?

GITTES
Where you were when your husband died.

EVELYN
. . . I can't tell you.

GITTES
You mean you don't know where you were?

EVELYN
I mean I can't tell you.

GITTES
—You were seeing someone too.

124 Evelyn looks squarely at him. She doesn't deny it.

GITTES
—For very long?

EVELYN
I don't see anyone for very long, Mr. Gittes. It's dif-
ficult for me. Now I think you know all you need to
about me. I didn't want publicity. I didn't want to
go into any of this, then or now. Is this all?

Gittes nods.

GITTES
Oh, by the way. What's the "c" stand for?

He's been fingering the envelope.

EVELYN
(she stammers slightly)
K . . . Cross.

GITTES

That your maiden name?

EVELYN

Yes . . . why?

GITTES

No reason.

Evelyn turns to Gittes.

EVELYN

You must've had a reason to ask me that.

GITTES
(shrugs)

No. I'm just a snoop.

EVELYN

You seem to have had a reason for every other question.

GITTES

No, not for that one.

EVELYN

I don't believe you.

Gittes suddenly turns sharply to Evelyn.

GITTES
(moving in)

Do me a favor. Sit still and act like I'm charming.

Evelyn involuntarily draws back.

GITTES
(continuing)

. . . There's somebody here. Say something. Anything. Something like we're being intimate.

125 Evelyn reluctantly allows Gittes to move closer and dangle his hand in front of their faces. She stares at him.

EVELYN
(meaning his nose)

How did it happen?

                          GITTES
                         (quietly)
Been meaning to talk to you about that.

                          EVELYN
                         (quietly)
Maybe putting your nose in other people's business?

                          GITTES
                         (quietly)
More like other people putting their business in my
nose.

Evelyn actually smiles a little.

                     WOMAN'S VOICE
You son of a bitch.

Gittes looks up and flashes his smile.

                          GITTES
Mrs. Match. How're you?

MRS. MATCH is swaying over the table, a plump woman with a glass of
whiskey in one hand, a large purse in the other, and a menacing look in
her eye.

                       MRS. MATCH
Don't give me that, you son of a bitch.

                          GITTES
    Okay.

Gittes turns back to Evelyn.

                          EVELYN
                         (softly)
Another satisfied client?

                          GITTES
Another satisfied client's wife.

                       MRS. MATCH
Look at me, you son of a bitch. You . . . you bastard.
Are you happy, are you happy now?

126 She tries to take a swipe at Gittes with her purse. Gittes covers himself. Waiters rush over.

                    MRS. MATCH
—You smug son of a bitch. My husband's so upset,
he sweats all night! How do you think that makes
me feel?

                    GITTES
Sweaty?

Mrs. Match swings at Gittes again and again. She catches him on the nose.
It hurts. He covers it, then swings his leg out from under the table and
deftly kicks her in the shin.

Mrs. Match drops her purse and spills her drink. She grabs her shin, hop-
ping around a little. The waiters who had tried to restrain her now try to
keep her from falling over.

                    GITTES
Let's get out of here before she picks up her purse.

They rise and move toward the door.

                    EVELYN
                    (quietly)
Tough guy, huh?

Gittes looks, sees she's kidding, and nods.

127 Outside in the Parking Lot—Dusk

Gittes' car has been brought by the parking attendant. The attendant
opens the passenger side for Evelyn.

                    EVELYN
Oh, no. I've got my own car. The cream-colored
Packard.

                    GITTES
                    (to attendant, who dutifully starts for her car)
Wait a minute, sonny.
                    (to Evelyn)
I think you better come with me.

                              EVELYN
What for? There's nothing more to say.
                          (to attendant)
Get my car, please.

The attendant starts after it again. Gittes leans on the open door of his car
and in to Evelyn. He talks quietly but spits it out.

                              GITTES
Okay, go home. But in case you're interested your
husband was murdered. Somebody's dumping tons
of water out of the city reservoirs when we're sup-
posedly in the middle of a drought, he found out,
and he was killed. There's a waterlogged drunk in
the morgue—involuntary manslaughter, if anybody
wants to take the trouble which they don't, it looks
like half the city is trying to cover it all up, which is
fine with me. But, Mrs. Mulwray—
                      (now inches from her)
I goddam near lost my nose! And I like it. I like
breathing through it. And I still think you're hiding
something.

Evelyn steadies herself on the open car door. She stares at Gittes for a long
moment. Then he gently tugs the car door closed.

                              EVELYN
Mr. Gittes—

He drives off into the Wilshire traffic, leaving Evelyn looking after him.

128 Int. DWP—Mulwray's Office Door

with its lettering HOLLIS I. MULWRAY, CHIEF ENGINEER.

Gittes goes through the door to the Secretary. She looks up. She recognizes
Gittes again and is not happy to see him.

                              GITTES
J. J. Gittes to see Mr. Yelburton.

The Secretary immediately gets up and goes into the inner office.

Gittes turns and strolls around the office a moment—he sees a photo-
graphic display of *The History of the DWP, The Early Years*, along the wall.
He stops as he spots a photo of the man with the cane Gittes had seen

photos of earlier. He is standing high in the mountains, near a pass. The
caption reads NOAH CROSS—1905. Cross is strikingly handsome.

Gittes immediately pulls out the envelope containing Evelyn's check. He
looks at the corner of it, his thumb pressing down under the middle initial
C, then he looks back to the photos—

The Secretary returns.

>   SECRETARY
> Mr. Yelburton will be busy for some time.

>   GITTES
> Well I'm on my lunch hour. I'll wait.

>   SECRETARY
> He's liable to be tied up indefinitely.

>   GITTES
> I take a long lunch. All day sometimes.

Gittes pulls out a cigarette case, offers the Secretary one. She refuses. He
lights up and begins to hum "The Way You Look Tonight," strolling
along the wall looking at more photographs.

129 Int. Mulwray's Offices

Here he spots several photos of a much younger Mulwray, along with
Noah Cross. One of the captions: HOLLIS MULWRAY AND NOAH CROSS AS
THE AQUEDUCT CLEARS THE SANTA SUSANNAH PASS—1912. Gittes, still
humming, turns to the Secretary.

>   GITTES
> Noah Cross worked for the Water Department?

>   SECRETARY
>   *(looking up)*
> Yes. No.

>   GITTES
>   *(humming, then)*
> He did or he didn't?

>   SECRETARY
> He owned it.

Gittes is genuinely surprised at this.

GITTES

He *owned* the Water Department?

SECRETARY

Yes.

GITTES

He owned the entire water supply for the city?

SECRETARY

Yes.

GITTES
(really surprised)
How did they get it away from him?

SECRETARY
(a sigh, then)
Mr. Mulwray felt the public should own the display—the water. If you'll just read the display—

GITTES
(glances back, hums, then)
Mr. Mulwray? I thought you said Mr. Cross owned the department.

SECRETARY
—Along with Mr. Mulwray.

GITTES

They were partners?

SECRETARY
(testily)
Yes. Yes, they were partners.

She gets up, annoyed, and goes into Yelburton's inner office.

Gittes goes back to the photographs. He hears a SCRATCHING SOUND, apparently coming from just outside the outer door.

He moves quickly to it, hesitates, swiftly opens the door. Workmen are behind it, scraping away Mulwray's name on the outer door, looking up at Gittes in some surprise.

The Secretary returns, sees the workman on the floor.

> SECRETARY
> *(to Gittes)*

Mr. Yelburton will see you now.

Gittes nods graciously, heads on into Yelburton's office.

130 Int. DWP—Yelburton & Gittes

There is a subtle but perceptible difference in Yelburton's attitude. He's now head of the department.

> YELBURTON
>
> Mr. Gittes, sorry to keep you waiting—these staff meetings, they just go on and on—

> GITTES
>
> Yeah—must be especially tough to take over under these circumstances.

> YELBURTON
>
> Oh, yes. Hollis was the best department head the city's ever had. My goodness, what happened to your nose?

> GITTES
> *(smiles)*
>
> I cut myself shaving.

> YELBURTON
>
> You ought to be more careful. That must really smart.

> GITTES
>
> Only when I breathe.

> YELBURTON
> *(laughing)*
>
> Only when you breathe . . . don't tell me you're still working for Mrs. Mulwray?

> GITTES
>
> I never was.

> YELBURTON
> *(stops smiling)*
>
> I don't understand.

GITTES

Neither do I, actually. But you hired me—or you hired that chippie to hire me.

YELBURTON

Mr. Gittes, you're not making a bit of sense.

GITTES

Well, look at it this way, Mr. Yelburton. Mulwray didn't want to build a dam—and he had a reputation that was hard to get around, so you decided to ruin it. Then he found out that you were dumping water every night—then he—was drowned.

YELBURTON

Mr. Gittes! That's an outrageous accusation. I don't know what you're talking about.

GITTES

Well, Whitey Mehrholtz over at the Times will. Dumping thousands of gallons of water down the toilet in the middle of a drought—that's news.

131 Gittes heads toward the door.

YELBURTON

Wait—please sit down, Mr. Gittes. We're . . . well, we're not anxious for this to get around, but we *have* been diverting a little water to irrigate avocado and walnut groves in the northwest valley. As you know, the farmers there have no legal right to our water, and since the drought we've had to cut them off—the city comes first, naturally. But, well, we've been trying to help some of them out, keep them from going under. Naturally, when you divert water—you get a little runoff.

GITTES

Yeah, a little runoff. Where are those orchards?

YELBURTON

I said, the northwest valley.

GITTES

That's like saying they're in Arizona.

> YELBURTON
>
> Mr. Gittes, my field men are out and I can't give you an exact location. . . .

Gittes nods.

> GITTES
>
> You're a married man, am I right?

> YELBURTON
>
> Yes.

> GITTES
>
> Hardworking, have a wife and kids . . .

> YELBURTON
>
> Yes . . .

> GITTES
>
> I don't want to nail you—I just want to know who put you up to it. I'll give you a few days to think it over—
>
> *(hands him a card)*
>
> —call me. I can help. Who knows? Maybe we can lay the whole thing off on a few big shots—and you can stay head of the department for the next twenty years.

Gittes smiles—leaves an unsmiling Yelburton.

132 Int. Gittes' Office

Gittes enters, drops his hat on Sophie's desk. Sophie tries to tell him something, but Gittes goes on into his office.

133 Evelyn Mulwray

is sitting, smoking. She looks up when he enters.

> EVELYN
>
> What's your usual salary?

Gittes moves to his desk, barely breaking stride at the sight of her.

                              GITTES

Thirty-five bucks daily for me, twenty for each of
my operators—plus expenses, plus my fee if I show
results.

He's sitting now. Evelyn is very pale now, obviously very shaken.

                              EVELYN

Whoever's behind my husband's death, why have
they gone to all this trouble?

                              GITTES

—Money. How they plan to make it by emptying
the reservoirs—that I don't know.

                              EVELYN

I'll pay your salary plus five thousand dollars if you
find out what happened to Hollis and who is involved.   •

Gittes buzzes Sophie.

                              GITTES

Sophie, draw up one of our standard forms for Mrs.
Mulwray.
                    (he leans back; to Evelyn)
Tell me, did you get married before or after Mul-
wray and your father sold the Water Department?

Evelyn nearly jumps at the question.

                              GITTES
                          (continuing)
Your father is Noah Cross, isn't he?

                              EVELYN

Yes, of course—it was quite a while after. I was just
out of grade school when they did that.

                              GITTES

—So you married your father's business partner?

Evelyn nods. She lights another cigarette.

GITTES

(continuing; staring at her, points to the ashtray)
You've got one going, Mrs. Mulwray.

EVELYN

—Oh.

134 She quickly stubs one out.

GITTES

Is there something upsetting about my asking about
your father?

EVELYN

No! . . . yes, a little. You see Hollis and my fa—my
father had a falling out. . . .

GITTES

Over the Water Department—or over you?

EVELYN

(quickly)
Not over me. Why would they have a falling out
over me?

GITTES

(noting her nervousness)
—Then it was over the Water Department.

EVELYN .

Not exactly. Well, I mean, yes. Yes and no. Hollis
felt the public should own the water, but I don't
think—my father felt that way. Actually, it was over
the Van der Lip. The dam that broke.

GITTES

—Oh, yeah?

EVELYN

Yes. He never forgave him for it.

GITTES

Never forgave him for what?

                            EVELYN

For talking him into building it, he never forgave
my father. . . . They haven't spoken to this day.

                            GITTES
                        (starts a little)

You sure about that?

                            EVELYN

Of course I'm sure.

                            GITTES

What about you—do you and your father get along?

**135 Sophie comes in with the form, cutting off Evelyn's reply. Gittes
places two copies on a coffee table in front of Evelyn.**

                            GITTES

Sign here . . . The other copy's for you.

She signs it. When she looks back up, Gittes is staring intently at her.

                            EVELYN

What are you thinking?

                            GITTES
        *(picking up one of copies, folding it, putting it in his
                            pocket)*

Before this—I turned on the faucet, it came out hot
and cold, I didn't think there was a thing to it.

136 Int. Seaplane

The engines make the small cabin vibrate. Gittes threads his way down
the tiny aisle of the eight-passenger cabin, which is full of middle-aged
men in old clothes and their fishing gear. Gittes is poked by a pole—has to
move along.

One of the old men says something to him.

                            GITTES
                        (above the engines)

What?

                            OLD MAN

You'll have to sit with the pilot.

Gittes moves forward into the cockpit. The PILOT looks up—nods for
Gittes to sit down, first moving a half-eaten cheese sandwich out of Gittes'
seat.

137 Ext. Harbor—Seaplane

taxiing down the ramp into the sea. In a moment it kicks up a spray of
foam and takes off.

138 Int. Cockpit

The island gradually looming larger before the Pilot and Gittes.

The Pilot glances over at Gittes—who, as usual, is impeccably dressed—a
contrast to the others on the plane.

> PILOT
> *(above the engines)*
> Well, you're not going fishing.

Gittes shakes his head.

> GITTES
> Not exactly.

> PILOT
> *(winks)*
> But that's what you told your wife—

The Pilot laughs raucously. Gittes laughs politely.

> PILOT
> Lots of fellas do. Tell the little woman they're going
> on a fishing trip, then shack up with some little twist
> on the island . . . she pretty?

> GITTES
> *(abruptly)*
> I'm going to see a man called Noah Cross—ever
> heard of him?

> PILOT
> Is the Pope Catholic? Who are you, mister? . . . I ask
> because he doesn't see a whole lot of people.

> GITTES
> I'm working for his daughter.

PILOT
(surprised)

That right? . . . She used to be some looker.

GITTES

She ain't exactly long in the tooth now.

PILOT

She must be about thirty-three, thirty-four.

GITTES

You must be thinking of a different daughter—

PILOT

No, he's only got one. I remember her age, I read it in the newspapers when she ran away.

GITTES

She ran away?

PILOT

Oh, yeah, it was a big thing at the time—Noah Cross' daughter. God Almighty. She was a wild little thing.

139 He gives a sidelong glance to Gittes, a little concerned he's said too much.

PILOT
(continuing)

'Course, she settled down nicely.

GITTES
(smiling a little)

Well, you never know, do you?

PILOT
(loosening up)

That's for sure.

GITTES

Why'd she run away?

PILOT

Oh, you know—she was sixteen or seventeen.

> GITTES
> *(nudging him)*
> We missed the best of it, didn't we, pal?

Both men laugh a little lewdly.

> PILOT
> She ran off to Mexico—rumor was she was knocked
> up and didn't even know who the father was—went
> there to get rid of it.

> GITTES
> You don't say?

> PILOT
> Cross was looking for her all over the country—of-
> fered rewards, everything. Felt real sorry for him,
> with all his money.

140 Albacore Club—Day

A pleasant but unobtrusive blue-and-white clapboard building on the bay
overlooking the harbor. The seaplane lands. A motor launch with a burgee of a fish flying from it turns and heads in the direction of the plane.

141 Ext. Winding Road—Rancho Del Cruce

Gittes, driven in a station wagon, passes under the sign with a cross
painted below the name.

The ranch itself is only partially in a valley on the island—as the wagon
continues one can SEE that it is actually a miniature California, encom-
passing desert, mountains, and canyon that tumble down palisades to the
windward side of the sea.

The wagon comes to a halt where a group of hands are clustered around a
corral. The circle of men drift apart, leaving NOAH CROSS standing,
using a cane for support, reedy but handsome in a rough linen shirt and
jeans. When he talks, his strong face is lively; in repose, it looks ravaged.

142 Ext. Bridle Path—Gittes & Cross

walking toward the main house—a classic Monterey. A horse led on a hal-
ter by another ranch hand slows down and defecates in the center of the
path they are taking. Gittes doesn't notice.

                          CROSS

Horseshit.

Gittes pauses, not certain he has heard correctly.

                          GITTES

Sir?

                          CROSS

I said horseshit.
                    (pointing)
Horseshit.

                          GITTES

Yes, sir, that's what it looks like—I'll give you that.

143 Cross pauses when they reach the dung pile. He removes his hat and waves it, inhales deeply.

                          CROSS

Love the smell of it. A lot of people do, but of course
they won't admit it. Look at the shape.

Gittes glances down out of politeness.

                          CROSS
        (continuing; smiling, almost enthusiastic)
Always the same.

Cross walks on. Gittes follows.

                          GITTES
                (not one to let it go)
Always?

                          CROSS

What? Oh, damn near—yes. Unless the animal's
sick or something.
                (stops and glances back)
—and the steam rising off it like that in the morning—that's life, Mr. Gittes. Life.

They move on.

CROSS

(continuing)

Perhaps this preoccupation with horseshit may seem a little perverse, but I ask you to remember this—one way or another, it's what I've dealt in all my life. Let's have breakfast.

144 Ext. Courtyard Veranda—Gittes & Cross at Breakfast

Below them is a corral where hands take Arabians, one by one, and work them out, letting them run and literally kick up their heels. Cross' attention is diverted by the animals from time to time. An impeccable Mexican butler serves them their main course, broiled fish.

CROSS

You know, you've got a nasty reputation, Mr. Gittes. I like that.

GITTES
(dubious)

Thanks.

CROSS

If you were a bank president, that would be one thing—but in your business it's admirable. And it's good advertising.

GITTES

It doesn't hurt.

CROSS

It's why you attract a client like my daughter.

GITTES

Probably.

CROSS

But I'm surprised you're still working for her—unless she's suddenly come up with another husband.

GITTES

No—she happens to think the last one was murdered.

Cross is visibly surprised.

CROSS

How did she get that idea?

GITTES

I think I gave it to her.

Cross nods.

CROSS

Uh-huh—oh, I hope you don't mind. I believe they
should be served with the head.

**145 Gittes glances down at the fish, whose isinglass eye is glazed over
with the heat of cooking.**

GITTES

Fine, as long as you don't serve chicken that way.

CROSS
(laughs)
Tell me—what do the police say?

GITTES

They're calling it an accident.

CROSS

Who's the investigating officer?

GITTES

Lou Escobar—he's a lieutenant.

CROSS

Do you know him?

GITTES

Oh yes.

CROSS

Where from?

GITTES

—We worked Chinatown together.

CROSS

Would you call him a capable man?

GITTES

Very.

CROSS

Honest?

GITTES

—Far as it goes—of course he has to swim in the same water we all do.

CROSS

Of course—but you've got no reason to think he's bungled the case?

GITTES

None.

CROSS

That's too bad.

GITTES

Too bad?

CROSS

It disturbs me, Mr. Gittes. It makes me think you're taking my daughter for a ride—financially speaking, of course. How much are you charging her?

GITTES
(carefully)

My usual fee—plus a bonus if I come up with any results.

CROSS

Are you sleeping with her? Come, come, Mr. Gittes—you don't have to think about that to remember, do you?

Gittes laughs.

GITTES

If you want an answer to that question I can always put one of my men on the job. Good afternoon, Mr. Cross.

CROSS

Mr. Gittes! You're dealing with a disturbed woman who's lost her husband. I don't want her taken advantage of. Sit down.

                          GITTES

What for?

                          CROSS

—You may think you know what you're dealing
with—but believe me, you don't.

146 This stops Gittes. He seems faintly amused by it.

                          , CROSS

Why is that funny?

                          GITTES

It's what the D.A. used to tell me about Chinatown.

                          CROSS

Was he right?

Gittes shrugs.

                          CROSS
                       (continuing)
. . . Exactly what do you know about me, Mr. Gittes?

                          GITTES

Mainly that you're rich and too respectable to want
your name in the papers.

                          CROSS
                      (grunts, then)
'Course I'm respectable. I'm old. Politicians, ugly
buildings, and whores all get respectable if they last
long enough. I'll double whatever your fees are—
and I'll pay you ten thousand dollars if you can find
Hollis' girlfriend.

                          GITTES

His girlfriend?

                          CROSS

Yes, his girlfriend.

                          GITTES

You mean the little chippie he was with at the El
Macando?

CROSS

Yes. She's disappeared, hasn't she?

GITTES

—Yeah.

CROSS

Doesn't that strike you as odd?

GITTES

No. She's probably scared to death.

CROSS

Wouldn't it be useful to talk to her?

GITTES

Maybe.

CROSS

If Mulwray was murdered, she was probably one of
the last people to see him.

GITTES

You didn't see Mulwray much, did you?

CROSS

—No—

GITTES

—When was the last time?

**147 Cross starts to reply, then there's the SOUND of a MARIACHI BAND,
and some men in formation clear a bluff about a hundred yards off. They
are dressed like Spanish dons on horseback. For the most part they are fat
in the saddle and pass along in disordered review to the music.**

CROSS

Sheriff's gold posse . . . bunch of damn fools who
pay $5,000 apiece to the sheriff's reelection. I let 'em
practice up out here.

GITTES

—Yeah. Do you remember the last time you talked
to Mulwray?

Cross shakes his head.

CROSS

—At my age, you tend to lose track. . . .

GITTES

Well, it was about five days ago. You were outside
the Pig 'n Whistle—and you had one hell of an argument.

Cross looks to Gittes in some real surprise.

GITTES
(continuing)

I've got the photographs in my office—if they'll
help you remember. What was the argument about?

CROSS
(a long pause, then)

My daughter.

GITTES

What about her?

CROSS

Just find the girl, Mr. Gittes. I think she is fright-
ened, and I happen to know Hollis was fond of her.
I'd like to help her if I can.

GITTES

I didn't realize you and Hollis were so fond of each
other.

148 Cross looks hatefully at Gittes.

CROSS

Hollis Mulwray made this city—and he made me
a fortune. . . . We were a lot closer than Evelyn
realized.

GITTES

—If you want to hire me, I still have to know what
you and Mulwray were arguing about.

CROSS
(painfully)

Well . . . she's an extremely jealous person. I didn't
want her to find out about the girl.

GITTES

How did you find out?

CROSS

I've still got a few teeth in my head, Mr. Gittes—and a few friends in town.

GITTES

Okay—my secretary'll send you a letter of agreement. Tell me—are you worried about that girl, or what Evelyn might do to her?

CROSS

Just find the girl.

GITTES

I'll look into it—as soon as I check out some avocado groves.

CROSS

Avocado groves?

GITTES

We'll be in touch, Mr. Cross.

149 Int. Hall of Records—Day

Dark and quiet except for the whirring of fans. Gittes approaches one of the CLERKS at a desk.

GITTES

I'm a little lost—where can I find the plat books for the northwest valley?

The Clerk's droopy eyes widen a little.

CLERK

Part of it's in Ventura County. We don't have Ventura County in our Hall of Records.

Which is a snotty remark. Gittes smiles.

GITTES

I'll settle for L.A. County.

> CLERK
> *(regards him, then)*
Row twenty-three, section C.

The Clerk turns away abruptly. Gittes regards his back a moment, then goes to the stacks.

150 Through the Stacks

Gittes sees the Clerk turn to another, say something. The second clerk gets on the phone. Gittes watches a moment, then swiftly turns his attention to the stacks.

He hauls down the northwest valley volume, opens it. It's huge and there's a lot to go through.

The print itself makes him squint.

150A Insert Page

showing TRACT LOT PARCEL, even a METES AND BOUNDS designation where the description of the land parcel is long and hopelessly involved—e.g. '6,000 paces to Rio Seco, thence 7,000 paces to Loma Linda, etc.' These descriptions are old and faded—in the owners' column, however, there are *numerous* freshly typed names pasted over the prior owners.

151 Gittes

hauls the huge volume back to the Clerk's desk.

> GITTES
> *(to Clerk)*
Say . . . uh . . . sonny.

152 The Clerk turns sharply around.

> GITTES
> How come all these new names are pasted into the
> plat book?

> CLERK
> Land sales out of escrow are always recorded
> within the week.

Gittes looks a little surprised.

> GITTES
>
> Then these are all new owners?

> CLERK
>
> —That's right.

> GITTES
> *(astonished)*
>
> —But that means that most of the valley's been sold
> in the last few months.

> CLERK
>
> If that's what it says.

> GITTES
>
> Can I check one of these volumes out?

> CLERK
> *(quietly snotty)*
>
> Sir, this is not a lending library, it's the Hall of
> Records.

> GITTES
>
> Well, then—how about a ruler?

> CLERK
>
> A ruler?

> GITTES
>
> The print's pretty fine. I forgot my glasses. I'd like to
> be able to read across.

The exasperated Clerk reaches around, rummages, slaps a ruler on the
desk.

Gittes goes back to the stacks with the ruler. He opens the book, places the
ruler not horizontally but vertically.

153 Omitted

154 Insert Plat Book Northwest Valley

Beside the OWNER column he places the ruler, looks toward the clerks,
then swiftly rips down the page, tearing out a strip about two inches wide,
containing the owner's name and property description.

As he tears, he either sniffles or coughs—to cover the SOUND of the PAPER being ripped.

155 Ext. Road—Gittes Driving—Day

amidst a hail of shimmering dust and heat, parched and drying groves, narrower roads.

He passes a ramshackle home, next to a rotting orchard. There is a SOLD sign on the collapsing barn. Gittes stops—checks it against the names he had taken from the Hall of Records.

156 Old Stucco Buildings Farther On

and a few withered pepper trees. Gittes has paused at this dried-up inter-section. There is a SOLD sign on a drugstore. Gittes looks o.s.

Coming INTO VIEW above the arid fields is a spiraling cloud of purple smoke. Gittes heads in that direction.

157 Omitted

158 Gittes parks at the edge of the field. About twenty yards away is a man mounted on a strange machine, holding a lid off it—billowing lavender clouds are belching forth.

Several CHILDREN are watching the man at work.

> GITTES
> *(to one of the Children)*
> Say, pal, what's he doing?

> CHILD
> Making some rain.

Gittes nods, walks over to the man who is elaborately busying himself with the intricacies of his machine. He's aware of Gittes watching him.

> GITTES
> Well, you're just the man I'm looking for.

The Rainmaker now glances down at Gittes, who as usual is immaculately dressed.

GITTES

Some associates and I are thinking of buying property out here—of course, we're worried about the
rainfall.

The Rainmaker steps down.

RAINMAKER

No problem with me on the job.

GITTES

—Yeah.
(glancing around at the desolate, dry field)
Do you have any references?

159 Rainmaker & Gittes

RAINMAKER

City of La Habra Heights—filled an 800,000-gallon
reservoir with sixteen inches of rain in two days.

GITTES
(nods)
That's swell. But how about here?
(pulling out names from his pocket)
Ever worked for Robert Knox, Emma Dill, Clarence
Speer, Marian Parsons, or Jasper Lamar Crabb?

RAINMAKER

Never heard of 'em . . . new owners?

GITTES

—Yeah.

RAINMAKER
(climbing back up)
Lot of turnover these days. Better tell them to get in
touch with me if they want to hang on to their land.

GITTES

—Yeah, I'll do that.

160 Gittes, Driving

is now covered with a film of dust.

He reaches a fork in the dirt road. There are a couple of mailboxes.

Gittes takes this fork and begins a slow ascent.

As he does, the tops of a line of bright green trees can be SEEN, coming more and more INTO VIEW, row upon row of avocado and walnut groves, their foliage heavy. The few structures in the distance are white-washed and well kept, right down to the whitewashed stones that mark the pathway to the home. Towering above it all is a huge wooden water tank.

Gittes drives through a gate that has NO TRESPASSING and KEEP OUT—PRI-VATE PROPERTY signs neatly printed on it.

He drives down the road into the grove.

161 Gittes

pulls to a halt in the road flanking the orchard lanes. He puts the car in neutral, stares at the trees. By contrast with what he has seen, they are lush and beautiful, their heavy branches barely swaying in a light breeze.

Then a SHOTGUN BLAST abruptly strips bare the branches of the tree he'd been staring at.

162 Ext. Avocado Groves—Day

Gittes is shocked. He looks behind him. Riding on horseback down the field in the direction he had just driven is a red-faced MAN in overalls. His hat blows off his head. He does not, however, lose the shotgun he has just used. Gittes' lane of retreat is denied him. He guns the car and takes off down one of the orchard lanes.

163 Moving with Gittes

The dirt lane is rough. As Gittes nears the end of it, a younger MAN on a mule blocks the exit.

Gittes veers a sharp left, knocking a branch off one of the trees, heading down one of the cross lanes. Here he's pursued by a scraggly dog that nips at the tires. Gittes yells at it.

164 Angle on Grove

Two farmers on foot, one using a crutch, run down the lanes toward a dust trail rising above the trees. They've spotted it—clearly it's from Gittes' car.

This hide-and-seek chase between one man on horseback, one on a mule, and a couple on foot continues up and down and across the orchard lanes—until Gittes' front tire and radiator are ruptured by another SHOT-GUN BLAST.

Gittes' car veers off, scattering a stray gaggle of geese—and smacks into an avocado tree, shaking loose a barrage of the heavy fruit onto Gittes and the car.

Gittes immediately tries to get out through the branches over the back of his car, but he's pulled off it by one of the younger farmers—a huge brute who he begins to tussle with. The Crippled Farmer begins to bang Gittes on the back with his crutch. The two of them manage to pound Gittes to the ground within moments, where the Crippled Farmer continues to whack away at Gittes with the crutch.

The older Red-Faced Farmer with the shotgun and the Man on a mule ride up.

> RED-FACED FARMER
> All right, quit it! Quit now! Search the man, see if
> he's armed.

165 Gittes is hefted half off the ground, and the two younger Farmers spin him around, going through his clothes. Gittes is badly banged up and half out on his feet. They toss his wallet, his silver cigarette case, etc., on the ground.

> RED-FACED FARMER
> I said see if he's armed, not empty his pockets.

> BIG FARMER
> —He ain't armed.

Gittes leans against the back of his car, breathing heavily.

> RED-FACED FARMER
> All right, mister—who you with—Water Depart-
> ment or the real-estate office—

Gittes' back is to the Red-Faced Farmer. He has trouble catching his breath. The Crippled Farmer pokes him rudely in the back with his crutch. Gittes turns sharply.

> GITTES
> *(to Crippled Farmer)*
> Get away from me!

> CRIPPLED FARMER
> Answer him!

> GITTES
> Touch me with that thing again and you'll need a pair of them.

> BIG FARMER
> *(shoving Gittes)*
> Whyn't you pick on somebody your own size?

> RED-FACED FARMER
> I said cut that out! Give him a chance to say something.

Gittes looks up at the Red-Faced Farmer.

> GITTES
> *(reaching down for his wallet)*
> Name's Gittes—I'm a private investigator and I'm not with either one.

> RED-FACED FARMER
> Then what are you doing out here?

> GITTES
> —Client hired me to see . . . whether or not the Water Department's been irrigating your land.

> RED-FACED FARMER
> Irrigating my land?
> *(exploding)*
> The Water Department's been sending you people to blow up my water tanks! They threw poison down three of my wells! I call that a funny way to irrigate—who'd hire you for a thing like that?

166 Gittes reaches into his pocket—the paper's on the ground. He picks it up.

> GITTES
>
> Mrs. Evelyn Mulwray—

> BIG FARMER
>
> Mulwray? That's the son of a bitch who's done it to us.

> GITTES
>
> Mulwray's dead—you don't know what you're talking about, you dumb Oakie—

The Big Farmer takes a swing at Gittes. Gittes kicks him squarely in the nuts, knees him in the jaw after he's doubled up, and hits him solidly. The Crippled Farmer takes careful aim and brings his crutch down on the back of Gittes' head. Gittes is knocked to the ground and lies still beside the Big Farmer, who is writhing in agony in the dirt.

> RED-FACED FARMER
>
> Well—that's that.

167 Black Screen

There's a PURLING SOUND, which soon becomes defined into the SOUND OF VOICES talking quietly—about whether to move or not to move, doctors, etc.

168 Close—Evelyn Mulwray

is staring down at Gittes, who is lying in the farmers' screened-in porch. The Red-Faced Farmer, his wife, and the Big Farmer are there, along with the dog.

The Red-Faced Farmer's wife has set tea out. The farmers—all of them—now seem awkward and a little embarrassed.

169 Ext. Front Porch—Red-Faced Farmer's House—Reaction—Gittes—Dusk

He focuses on Evelyn, who sits right next to him. He's got dried blood down the side of his face from his nose, a huge mouse on his cheek, and his clothes are torn in a couple of spots.

> GITTES
> *(to Evelyn)*

What's going on?

> DUBOIS
> *(quietly, almost as if he were in a hospital)*
> You didn't look too good, so we thought we better
> call your employer.

Gittes nods. He checks his watch. He looks out—it's almost evening. Gittes says nothing. The wife of the Red-Faced Farmer (DUBOIS) looks reproachfully at Dubois. Gittes feels the back of his head. It obviously hurts him.

170 Ext. Dubois Farmhouse—Evening

Evelyn and Gittes go out to her car, the cream-colored Packard. Dubois accompanies them—along with the Big Farmer, who is carrying a crate of something. Gittes has cleaned himself up a little.

> DUBOIS
> —Look here, if it's all the same with you, we'll get
> your car patched up—if you'll tell me what your
> trousers run you, I'll make good on them, Mr.
> Gittes.

> GITTES

It's okay, Mr. Dubois.

> DUBOIS
> *(to Evelyn)*
> —It's just that they're after everybody out here,
> tearing up our irrigation ditches—trying to make
> our land worthless so they can pick it up for twenty-
> five dollars an acre—

Gittes nods.

> DUBOIS
> *(continuing)*
> Anyway—Earl here is sorry too. He wants to give
> you something to take back with you.

Gittes looks. Earl is holding a huge crate brimful of avocados.

GITTES

Thanks, Earl.

171 Int. Car—Evelyn & Gittes—Dusk

Evelyn driving.

GITTES

Thanks for coming . . .

Gittes pulls out cigarette case, takes one, offers one to Evelyn, who refuses.

GITTES

—That dam is a con job.

EVELYN

What dam?

GITTES

The one your husband opposed—they're conning
L.A. into building it, only the water won't go to
L.A.—it'll go here.

EVELYN

The Valley?

GITTES

Everything you can see, everything around us—I
was at the Hall of Records today—
        (whips out papers, turns on the car light)
—That bother you?

EVELYN

No.

GITTES

        (looking over papers)
In the last three months, Robert Knox has bought
7,000 acres, Emma Dill 12,000 acres, Clarence Speer
5,000 acres, and Jasper Lamar Crabb 25,000 acres.

EVELYN

Jasper Lamar Crabb?

GITTES

Know him?

                              EVELYN
No, I think I'd remember.

                              GITTES
Yeah—they've been blowing these farmers out of
here and buying their land for peanuts—Have any
idea what this land'll be worth with a steady water
supply? About thirty million more than they paid.

                              EVELYN
—And Hollis knew about it?

                              GITTES
It's why he was killed—Jasper Lamar Crabb—Jasper Lamar Crabb—

He's pulling out his wallet, excitedly now, spilling its contents onto the
seat. He pulls out the obituary column he'd folded up earlier in the day.

                              GITTES
                           (continuing)
We got it. We got it, baby.

                              EVELYN
What? What is it?

                              GITTES
There was a memorial service at the Mar Vista Inn
today for Jasper Lamar Crabb. He died three weeks
ago.

                              EVELYN
Is that unusual?

                              GITTES
Two weeks ago he bought those 25,000 acres. That's
unusual.

172 Ext. Mar Vista Inn and Rest Home—Night

Evelyn's car pulls up before the elegant Spanish rest home, its entryway
illuminated by streetlights. There is a small sign giving the name of the
place in elegant neon scroll. It sits on the rolling green lawns.

Gittes gets out of the car with Evelyn. He offers her his arm, and they go
up the walkway to the entrance.

173 Int. Mar Vista Inn and Rest Home

Gittes and Evelyn are approached by an unctuous man in his forties with a flower in his buttonhole. He sees Evelyn first.

> PALMER
>
> Hello there, I'm Mr. Palmer. Can I help you folks?

Then he gets a clear look at Gittes—bruised, trousers torn, etc.

> GITTES
>
> Yes, I sure hope so. It's Dad—
> *(indicating his disheveled appearance)*
> —I just can't handle him anymore, can I, sweet-heart?

Evelyn shakes her head.

> PALMER
>
> Oh, my goodness.

> GITTES
> *(hastily)*
> Nothing to do with Dad. It's me, actually.

> EVELYN
>
> They just don't get along very well. Dad's a lamb with anyone else.

> PALMER
> *(not so sure)*
> Oh—well—I don't know—

> GITTES
>
> Naturally, I want the best for him, money is no object.

> PALMER
>
> —Perhaps if we could meet your father—

> GITTES
>
> There's just one question.

> PALMER
>
> Of course.

> GITTES
>
> Do you accept anyone of the Jewish persuasion?

Evelyn can't quite conceal her surprise at the question.

> PALMER
> *(very embarrassed)*
>
> I'm sorry—we don't.

> GITTES
> *(smoothly)*
>
> Don't be sorry, neither does Dad. Wanted to make
> sure though, didn't we, honey?

174 Evelyn stares back at Gittes, amused and appalled. She manages to nod.

> GITTES
>
> Just to be certain, I wonder if you could show us a
> list of your patients?

> PALMER
> *(polite but pointed)*
>
> We don't reveal the names of our *guests* as a matter
> of policy. I know you'd appreciate that if your father
> came to live with us.

Gittes locks eyes with Palmer.

> GITTES
> *(confidentially)*
>
> That's exactly what we wanted to hear.

> PALMER
>
> Oh, good.

> GITTES
>
> I wonder, is it too late for us to have a look around?

> PALMER
>
> I don't think so—be happy to show you—

> GITTES
>
> Would you mind if we took a stroll on our own?

> PALMER

—Just, if you will, confine yourself to the main building—it's nearly bedtime.

> GITTES

We understand, c'mon, sweetheart.

He takes Evelyn.

175 Int. Parlor—Evelyn

looking. Either by accident or design, the primarily octogenarian guests have segregated themselves. In one wing the men are playing pinochle, some are playing dominoes. One elderly gentleman sits by himself carefully peeling an orange.

In an adjacent parlor several white-headed ladies work on a quilt.

Gittes grabs Evelyn's hand.

> GITTES
> *(quietly)*

They're all here. Every goddam name.

Gittes points to the wall—it reads ACTIVITIES BOARD. There are titles—LAWN BOWLING, BRIDGE, FISHING, CROQUET—below them are the names of the guests, entered under certain activities, for certain days.

After Evelyn looks, she turns to Gittes.

> GITTES
> *(continuing; indicating the ancients around them)*

You're looking at the owners of a 50,000-acre empire.

> EVELYN
> *(astonished)*

They can't be.

> GITTES

They may not know it—but they are.

176 Gittes strolls toward the women knitting and working on the quilt.

> GITTES
>
> Hello, girls.

Two of the ladies giggle. The third continues to busy herself with her quilt, off by herself.

> GITTES
> *(continuing)*
> Which one of you is Emma Dill?

Two of them say, "She is," and point in different directions. The third gives them a curt look and goes back to her knitting. Gittes approaches her.

> GITTES
>
> Are you Emma?

Some old voice is singing softly, "Don't Sit Under the Apple Tree."

> EMMA
>
> —Yes.

> GITTES
>
> I've been wanting to meet you.

> EMMA
>
> Why?

> GITTES
>
> —Did you know that you're a very wealthy woman?

> EMMA
> *(stitching, smiles)*
> —I'm not.

> GITTES
>
> Well you own a lot of land.

> EMMA
>
> Not anymore. Oh, some time ago my late husband owned a good deal of beach property in Long Beach—but we lost it.

Gittes looks at the quilt. In it is the head of a fish—among the rest of the crazy quilt pattern. Gittes spots it.

GITTES

That's just lovely.

EMMA

Thank you. . .

177 He looks through the quilt for other pieces of the fish—comes across the tail—and by it—the Initials A. C.

GITTES
(indicating tail)
—Where did you get this material?

EMMA
(what it sounds like)
The apple-core club—

GITTES

—The apple core?

EMMA

No—the *albacore*. It's a fish. My grandson's a member—and they take very nice care of us.

GITTES

How do they do that?

EMMA

Give us things—not just some old flag like this, but . . .

GITTES
(kneeling)

But what?

PALMER'S VOICE

We're a sort of unofficial charity of theirs, Mr. Gittes. Would you care to come this way? Someone wants to see you.

Gittes looks up, sees Palmer standing in the doorway, looking taut and a little drawn. Evelyn is beside him. She gestures, as if there's someone behind Palmer.

Gittes rises.

> GITTES

See you later, Emma.

He walks toward Palmer, who waits for him to walk in front.

178 At the Entrance Hall—Mulvihill

is waiting. He's got his hand in his pocket. Evelyn looks to Gittes. The four
of them stand there, Mulvihill towering over everyone.

> MULVIHILL

Come on—I want you to meet somebody, Gittes.

> GITTES
> *(glancing from Palmer to Mulvihill)*

Can—we leave the lady out of this?

> MULVIHILL
> *(a little uncertain)*

—Yeah, why not?

> GITTES

Okay, I'd like to walk her to her car.

> EVELYN

I'll stay.

> GITTES
> *(taking her by the arm)*

Get in the car.

> MULVIHILL

I'll see she makes it.

Mulvihill has walked up beside Gittes. He makes the mistake of opening
the glass door in the entryway, putting his back to Gittes for a moment.
Gittes swiftly pulls Mulvihill's jacket up over his head. He spins him
around. With his jacket covering his face, Gittes hammers away at Mulvihill, beating him against the glass door, along the wall, mercilessly
pounding his fists into the cloth until the cloth turns red and Mulvihill
begins to sink to the red-tile floor. Palmer screams. Evelyn stands there,
astonished. Mulvihill's gun has clattered to the floor.

GITTES
(as Mulvihill hits the floor, to Evelyn)
What are you waiting for? Get in the car!

Evelyn goes.

179 Mulvihill tries to get up again. Palmer starts to go for the gun, nearly picking it up. Gittes slaps it out of his hand and kicks it. It goes flying down the hall at least thirty feet, hits the wall. Palmer goes screaming off into the night. Gittes turns back to Mulvihill, who starts to get up, then collapses.

Gittes goes out the front door, ignoring the excited audience of ancients behind him.

180 Outside

As Gittes walks down the pathway he stops—two men are coming toward him. One of them is shorter and has the nervous, jerky movements of the man who slit his nose.

Gittes stops. The two men fan out and continue to move toward him. Gittes spots the two-tone shoes. He begins to back up.

Suddenly there is a pair of headlights flashing brilliantly behind the two men. In a moment Evelyn's car is headed across the lawn directly toward the two men, accelerating as it gets near them. They look in disbelief, then dive for safety. The car skids to a stop, fishtailing a little on the grass.

Evelyn opens the passenger door.

EVELYN
Get in.

Gittes jumps in, and she takes off across the lawn, tilting the elegant little neon sign on the lawn as she goes. Two SHOTS ARE FIRED.

181 Int. Car—Evelyn & Gittes

Evelyn looking straight ahead, driving. After a moment she takes one hand off the wheel and rubs her left eye a little. Gittes watches her. He smiles.

182 Ext. Veranda, Mulwray Home—Night

Gittes stands on the veranda, smoking a cigarette, staring off into the night.

Evelyn comes out to the veranda carrying a tray with whiskey and an ice bucket on it. She sets it down—Gittes turns.

> GITTES
> *(watching her pour)*
> Maid's night off?

> EVELYN
> —Why?

> GITTES
> *(a little surprised, he laughs)*
> What do you mean, "why"? Nobody's here, that's all.

> EVELYN
> *(handing Gittes his drink)*
> —I gave everybody the night off—

> GITTES
> —Easy, it's an innocent question.

> EVELYN
> No question from you is innocent, Mr. Gittes.

> GITTES
> *(laughing)*
> I guess not—to you, Mrs. Mulwray. Frankly you really saved my a—my neck tonight.

They drink.

> EVELYN
> Tell me something—does this usually happen to you, Mr. Gittes?

> GITTES
> What's that, Mrs. Mulwray?

> EVELYN

—Well, I'm only judging on the basis of one afternoon and an evening, but if that's how you go about
your work, I'd say you're lucky to get through a
whole day.

> GITTES
> *(pouring himself another drink)*

—Actually, this hasn't happened to me in some
time.

> EVELYN

—When was the last time?

> GITTES

Why?

> EVELYN

Just—I don't know why. I'm asking.

Gittes touches his nose, winces a little.

> GITTES

It was in Chinatown.

> EVELYN

What were you doing there?

> GITTES
> *(taking a long drink)*

—Working for the District Attorney.

> EVELYN

Doing what?

183 Gittes looks sharply at her. Then:

> GITTES

As little as possible.

> EVELYN

The District Attorney gives his men advice like that?

> GITTES

They do in Chinatown.

She looks at him. Gittes stares off into the night.

Evelyn has poured herself another drink.

> EVELYN
> Bothers you to talk about it, doesn't it?

Gittes gets up.

> GITTES
> No—I wonder—could I—do you have any peroxide
> or something?

He touches his nose lightly.

> EVELYN
> Oh sure. C'mon.

She takes his hand and leads him back into the house.

184 Int. Bathroom—Mirror

Gittes pulls the plaster off his nose, stares at it in the mirror. Evelyn takes some hydrogen peroxide and some cotton out of a medicine cabinet. Evelyn turns Gittes' head toward her. She has him sit on the pullman tile adjacent to the sink.

> EVELYN
> Doctor did a nice job . . .

She begins to work on his nose with the peroxide. Then she sees his cheek—checks back in his hair.

> EVELYN
> *(continuing)*
> —Boy, oh boy, you're a mess—

> GITTES
> —Yeah—

> EVELYN
> *(working on him)*
> —So why does it bother you to talk about it . . .
> Chinatown . . .

> GITTES

—Bothers everybody who works there—but to me—it was—bad luck.

Gittes shrugs.

> EVELYN

—Hold still—why?

> GITTES

—You can't always tell what's going on there—

> EVELYN

. . . No—why was it—unlucky?

> GITTES

—I thought I was keeping someone from being hurt, and actually I ended up making sure they were hurt.

> EVELYN

Could you do anything about it?

185 They're very close now as she's going over a mouse very near his eye.

> GITTES

Yeah—make sure I don't find myself in Chinatown anymore. Wait a second—

He takes hold of her and pulls her even closer.

> EVELYN
> *(momentarily freezing)*

—What's wrong?

> GITTES

Your eye.

> EVELYN

What about it?

> GITTES
> *(staring intently)*

There's something black in the green part of your eye.

> EVELYN
> *(not moving)*
> . . . Oh, that . . . it's a flaw in the iris. . . .

> GITTES

. . . A flaw . . .

> EVELYN
> *(she almost shivers)*
> . . . Yes . . . sort of a birthmark. . . .

Gittes kisses her lightly, gradually rises until he's standing, holding her. She hesitates, then wraps her arms around him.

186 Int. Mulwray Bedroom—Telephone

on a nightstand, city lights visible through the open window behind it. It is RINGING. Evelyn's arm reaches INTO SHOT. SOUND of something hitting the headboard. Gittes moans.

VIEW SHIFTS TO INCLUDE Gittes in bed, holding his head, which he's just hit. Evelyn pauses in her reach to the phone. She turns to him, whispers, "I'm sorry," kisses him on the head and lips. PHONE CONTINUES TO RING. She picks it up.

> EVELYN

. . . Hello . . .

> *(in Spanish now)*
> . . . No, no, I'll come and help, just keep watching
> her and don't do anything until I get there. . . . 'bye.

VIEW SHIFTS AGAIN TO INCLUDE Gittes in bed, watching Evelyn next to him as she's talking on the phone. She hangs up. She touches Gittes' cheek lightly.

> EVELYN

I have to go.

Gittes stares at her silently.

> GITTES

Where?

> EVELYN

—Just—I have to.

GITTES

And I want to know where.

EVELYN

(she starts out of bed)

Please don't be angry. . . . Believe me, it's got nothing to do with you—

GITTES

(stopping her)

Where are you going?

EVELYN

(near tears)

Please! . . . Trust me this much. . . .

(she kisses him lightly)

I'll be back—look, there is something I should tell
you. The fishing club that old lady mentioned, the
pieces of the flag—

GITTES

The Albacore Club.

EVELYN

It has to do with my father.

GITTES

I know.

EVELYN

He owns it. You know?

GITTES

I saw him.

EVELYN

(sitting up straight)

You *saw* my fa—father? When?

GITTES

This morning.

EVELYN

(panicked)

You didn't tell me.

GITTES

There hasn't been a lot of time.

187 She leaps out of bed, throwing on a robe.

EVELYN

What did he say?

(insistent)

What did he say?

GITTES

—That you were jealous, and he was worried about
what you might do.

EVELYN

Do? To who?

GITTES

Mulwray's girlfriend, for one thing. He wanted to
know where she was.

Evelyn starts quickly for the bathroom, then comes back and kneels by the
side of the bed, takes Gittes' hand.

EVELYN

I want you to listen to me—my father is a very dangerous man. You don't know how dangerous. You
don't know how crazy.

GITTES

Give me an example.

EVELYN

You may think you know what's going on, but you
don't.

GITTES

That's what your father said—you're telling me he's
in back of this whole thing?

EVELYN

It's possible.

GITTES

Including the death of your husband?

EVELYN

It's *possible*. Please don't ask me any more questions
now. Just wait, wait for me—I'll be back. I need you
here.

She kisses him, rushes to the bathroom, shuts the door. Gittes stares at it a
moment. Then leaps out of bed, rummages around, tosses on his trousers.
He grabs his shoes, throws them on. Then hurries out of the bedroom.

188 Ext. Mulwray Home—Gittes

running across the driveway to the garage. There are two cars there—
Mulwray's Buick and Evelyn's Packard.

Gittes moves over to the Buick, opens the passenger door.

189 Int. Buick—Gittes

checks the ignition. No key is in it. He pulls a couple of wires from under
the dash, starts to mess with them, seems satisfied. Slides out across the
seat, slams the door.

190 Ext. Mulwray Driveway—Night

Gittes hurries over to the Packard. He gets down on the driveway, lying
on his back, bracing himself. With the heel of his shoe he kicks at the right
rear taillight of the car. He shatters the red lens, gets up. He carefully pulls
the red lens off the taillight, exposing the white light beneath it. He tosses
the red lens into the shrubbery and hurries back toward the house.

191 One Red and One White Taillight—Moving—Night

Evelyn's car speeds along the curves on Sunset Boulevard, the red-and-
white lights coming IN AND OUT OF VIEW.

192 Gittes Driving—Night

behind the wheel of Mulwray's car, keeping a healthy distance from Evelyn in front of him.

193 Evelyn's Packard

pulls up before a small little bungalow. She gets out, looks up and down
the street. There is nothing. She hurries on up the walkway to the front
door.

194 Down the Street—Gittes in Buick

idles the engine with the lights off. He brings the car a few yards farther down the street, parking it near Evelyn's.

Gittes gets out of the car and goes up the walkway. The curtains are drawn except for one of the small windows on the side of the house. He goes to it and looks, balancing on the edge of the porch.

195 Through the Window

Gittes sees Evelyn's Oriental servant rush through the living room of the small house. In a moment he reemerges back through the living room carrying a tray with a glass and pitcher on it.

196 Gittes

around to the side of the house. He runs into shrubbery and a short picket fence.

He climbs over it, follows along the stucco wall to a series of windows at the corner of the house. These all have shades on them. He can hear someone crying in the house. Someone else talking alternately firmly and plaintively in Spanish. Here the windows have blinds. He moves to one where the blind is not completely drawn—there's an inch or so of space at the bottom.

197 Through the Window

Gittes can see the servant again. Evelyn is packing back and forth in and out of his line of vision. After a moment someone rises INTO SHOT—obviously from lying on a bed. The figure is just a few feet from Evelyn. Her tearstained face comes INTO VIEW. It is unmistakably the girl Gittes had last seen with Hollis Mulwray. Mulwray's girlfriend. She's looking up to Evelyn, speaking in Spanish. Her words are not discernible but the tone is—bitter, anguished. A newspaper is strewn about the room.

Evelyn kneels. She insists that the girl swallow down some pills. The girl reluctantly does.

198 Gittes

continues to watch.

199 Ext. Street—Evelyn—Night

emerges from the house, goes to her car, and gets in.

200 Int. Car

Evelyn sees Gittes sitting in her car, staring coldly at her.

> GITTES
>
> Okay, give me the keys.

> EVELYN
> *(stunned, furious)*
>
> You bastard.

> GITTES
>
> —It's either that or you drive to the police yourself.

> EVELYN
>
> The police?

> GITTES
>
> C'mon, Mrs. Mulwray—you've got your husband's
> girlfriend tied up in there!

> EVELYN
>
> She's not tied up!

> GITTES
>
> You know what I mean. You're keeping her there
> against her will.

> EVELYN
>
> I am not!

> GITTES
>
> Then let's go talk to her.

201 Gittes starts to get out of the car. Evelyn grabs his arm, nearly screaming.

> EVELYN
>
> No!

Her intensity actually rips Gittes' already partially torn jacket. He looks at
it and her. It seems to have a momentary calming effect on both of them.

                          EVELYN
                        (continuing)
She's too upset.

                          GITTES
What about?

                          EVELYN
Hollis' death. I tried to keep it from her. I didn't
want her upset before I could make plans for her to
leave.

                          GITTES
You mean she just found out?

                          EVELYN
. . . Yes.

                          GITTES
That's not what it looks like, Mrs. Mulwray.

                          EVELYN
What does it look like?

                          GITTES
Like she knows about Hollis' death—like she knows
more than you want her to tell.

                          EVELYN
You're insane.

Gittes explodes.

                          GITTES
Just tell me the truth—*I'm* not the police. *I* don't care
what you've done. I'm not going to hurt you—but
one way or another I'm going to know.

                          EVELYN
You won't go to the police if I tell you?

                          GITTES
I will if you don't.

A long pause. Evelyn's head sinks onto the steering wheel, her hair covering her face.

EVELYN

She's my sister.

202 Evelyn is breathing very deeply now—not crying, but the kind of deep breathing that comes from real hysteria. Gittes puts an arm on her shoulder.

GITTES

Take it easy. . . . If it's your sister it's your sister . . . why all the secrecy?

She lifts her head and looks up at him. He's genuinely puzzled.

EVELYN
(really upset)

I can't . . .

GITTES

Because of Hollis? Because she was seeing your husband? Was that it? Jesus Christ, say something. Was that it?

She nods. Gittes sighs.

EVELYN
(finally)

I would never, ever have harmed Hollis. I loved him more than my own family. He was the most gentle, decent man imaginable . . . and he put up with more from me than you'll ever know. . . . I just wanted him to be happy. . . .

She begins to cry softly.

GITTES
(after a moment)

—I took your husband's Buick . . .
(he opens the car door)
I'll return it tomorrow.

EVELYN

Aren't you coming back with me?

GITTES

—Don't worry. I'm not telling anybody about this.

                                    EVELYN
      . . . That's not what I meant.

There is a long moment of silence. Gittes looks over to Evelyn. Her hair
covers most of her face from him.

                                    GITTES
                                    (finally)
      . . . Yeah, well . . . I'm very tired, Mrs. Mulwray.
      Good night.

He gets out and slams the car door. She drives off.

203 Int. Shower—Gittes' Apartment—Gittes

The spray is hitting him full on the top of the head. Gittes is so exhausted,
he's literally holding on to the nozzle as the water pours down. He shuts
the shower off, reaches weakly for a towel—dabs his nose lightly with it.

204 Int. Gittes' Bedroom—Gittes

pads around in elegant silk pajamas.

He walks over to the window where morning light is streaming in. He
closes the curtains, collapses on the bed, on top of the covers, inert. Almost
immediately the PHONE RINGS. Gittes lets it go on for a moment, then
picks it up without saying anything.

                              VOICE ON PHONE
                                    (male)
      Gittes? . . . Gittes?

                                    GITTES
      —Yeah.

                              VOICE ON PHONE
      Ida Sessions wants to see you.

                                    GITTES
      Who?

                              VOICE ON PHONE
      Ida Sessions. You remember Ida.

Gittes slowly rises to one elbow.

> GITTES
> —Yeah? . . . I do?

> VOICE ON PHONE
> Sure you do.

> GITTES
> —Well, tell you what, pal. If Ida wants to see me,
> she can call me—at my office.

He hangs up, falls back down. PHONE RINGS AGAIN. AND AGAIN.
Gittes swears, picks it up.

> VOICE ON PHONE
> 684½ East Tensington—Echo Park. She begged me
> to call. She's waiting for you.

Before Gittes can say anything, phone clicks dead.

205 Ext. Cerritos Tower Road—Hollywood Hills—Early Morning

Gittes pulls up. It is a bungalow courtyard with a very narrow walkway
and sickly green stucco.

206 Ext. Ida Sessions' Apartment—Day

Gittes at the front door. It's slightly ajar. He knocks. Nothing. He opens it
and enters.

207 Int. Living Room

Morning light filters through the half-open blinds. Dust particles in the
shafts of light. It's still and empty. Gittes sees something down the hall,
under the legs of a telephone table. Gittes moves toward it. It is grotesque.
When he gets closer, he can see it's a wilted head of lettuce. Just inside the
kitchen some radishes and onions lie on the linoleum. Gittes walks on into
the kitchen.

208 Int. Kitchen

Clearing the kitchen counter, Gittes sees IDA SESSIONS lying on her back
on the floor, surrounded by the groceries from a broken bag. Ice cream has
melted around her. Her eyes are open; a stream of ants is moving across
the ice cream and into her mouth. She's recognizable as the woman who
posed as Evelyn Mulwray.

Gittes kneels over her. He gingerly opens her handbag, fishes for its contents, takes them, and looks at them on the kitchen counter—wallet with a few bills in it, driver's license with her name, a Screen Actors Guild card. Gittes nods, turns, carefully replaces the items in the purse.

He idly opens the broom closet, pantry, and even Frigidaire, which is all but empty. Then he steps over her body and moves across the hall to a door that is slightly ajar.

209 Int. Bathroom

Gittes enters and turns on the light.

> ESCOBAR
> Find anything interesting, Gittes?

Escobar and another PLAINCLOTHESMAN stand in the bathroom by the entrance to the bedroom door. Gittes turns around. A THIRD MAN is now coming down the hall from the bedroom.

Gittes looks at the two, doesn't reply.

> ESCOBAR
> What are you doing here?

> GITTES
> Didn't you call?

> ESCOBAR
> *(jerk of his head toward the kitchen)*
> How do you happen to know her?

> GITTES
> I don't.

> ESCOBAR
> *(turning toward the other room)*
> —Let me show you something.

210 Int. Kitchen

Escobar points to the number MU 7279 on the side of one of the kitchen cabinets.

> ESCOBAR
> Isn't that your number?

GITTES

Is it? I forget. I don't call myself that often.

ESCOBAR

Just to be on the safe side, we had Loach here give
you a ring.

He indicates one of his Assistants.

LOACH
(a slight sneer)

What happened to your nose, Gittes? Somebody
slam a bedroom window on it?

GITTES
(right back, smiling)

Nope, your wife got excited, crossed her legs a little
too quick. You understand, pal.

The Assistant starts to move for Gittes, who is ready for him. Escobar
steps between the two.

ESCOBAR
(to other Assistant)

Loach.

(Escobar pulls out a drawer)

How about these? Look familiar?

In the open drawer are the photos of Mulwray and the girl in the park, on
a boat, and at the El Macando on the veranda.

GITTES
(no point in denying it)

Yeah, I took 'em. So what?

ESCOBAR

How did *she*—

(meaning the corpse)

—happen to have them?

Gittes takes a deep breath.
Escobar nods.

ESCOBAR

You really think I'm stupid, don't you, Gittes?

GITTES

I don't think about it one way or the other. But if
you want, give me a day or two and I'll get back to
you. Now I'd like to go home.

ESCOBAR

I want the rest of the pictures.

GITTES

What pictures?

ESCOBAR
(meaning corpse)
This broad hired you, Gittes, not Evelyn Mulwray.

GITTES

Yeah?

ESCOBAR

Yeah—somebody wanted to shake down Mulwray,
she hired you, and that's how you happen to know
Mulwray was murdered.

GITTES

I heard it was an accident.

ESCOBAR

C'mon, you think you're dealing with a bunch of
assholes? Mulwray had salt water in his goddam
lungs! Now how did he get that in a freshwater
reservoir?

**211 Gittes is surprised at this piece of information but remains non-
plussed.**

ESCOBAR

You followed him night and day. You saw who
killed him. You took pictures of it. It was Evelyn
Mulwray—she's been paying you off like a slot machine ever since her husband died.

GITTES
(smiling)
You accusing me of extortion?

ESCOBAR

Absolutely.

GITTES

—I don't think I need a day or two—you're even dumber than you think I think you are. Not only that, I'd never extort a nickel out of my worst enemy. That's where I draw the line, Escobar.

ESCOBAR

Yeah, I once knew a whore who for enough money would piss in a customer's face—but she'd *never* shit on his chest. That's where she drew the line.

GITTES
(smiling)

Well, I hope she wasn't too much of a disappointment to you, Lou.

Escobar manages a thin smile.

ESCOBAR

I want those photographs, Gittes. We're talking about accessory after the fact, conspiracy, and extortion—minimum.

GITTES

Why do you think Mulwray's body was moved, you dimwit? Evelyn Mulwray knocked off her husband in the ocean—and thought it would look like more of an accident if she hauled him up to the Oak Pass Reservoir?

This is a little telling.

GITTES
(continuing)

Mulwray was murdered and moved—because somebody didn't want his body found in the ocean.

ESCOBAR

And why's that?

> GITTES
>
> He found out somebody was dumping water there.
> That's what they were trying to cover up by moving
> him.

This stops Escobar. He's dumbfounded by it.

> ESCOBAR
>
> What are you talking about?

> GITTES
>
> C'mon, I'll show you.

Escobar hesitates.

> GITTES
> (continuing)
>
> C'mon—make a decision, Lou. You're in charge.

The men around Escobar look to him. Escobar nods grudgingly.

212 Close Shot—Storm Drain

It yawns AT CAMERA, only a trickle of water dropping into the ocean.

VIEW WIDENS TO INCLUDE Escobar, Gittes, and two Plainclothesmen, standing and staring at the empty pipe as if they expect it to talk.

> GITTES
> (squinting in sunlight)
>
> It's too late.

> ESCOBAR
>
> Too late for what?

> GITTES
>
> They only dump the water at night.

213 A THIRD ASSISTANT runs down the side of the cliff and over to Escobar.

> ESCOBAR
>
> Reach anybody?

> THIRD ASSISTANT
>
> Yelburton, he's the new chief.

ESCOBAR

I know who he is. Well?

THIRD ASSISTANT

He says—

GITTES

I *know* what he says.

ESCOBAR
(to Gittes)

Shut up.

(to Assistant)

Go on.

THIRD ASSISTANT

Yelburton says they're irrigating in the valley—
there's always a little runoff when they do that. And
he says Gittes knows that, and has been going
around making irresponsible accusations all week.

Escobar turns to Gittes. Stares at him for a long moment.

ONE OF ASSISTANTS

Let's swear out a warrant for her arrest. What are
we waiting for?

GITTES
(meaning Escobar)

Because he just made lieutenant and he wants to
hang on to his little gold bar.

Escobar stares hatefully at Gittes.

ESCOBAR

Have your client in my office in two hours—and remember, I've got you for withholding evidence
right now.

214 Ext. Mulwray Home—Day

Gittes, in Mulwray's Buick, whips into the driveway. He looks in the garage. Evelyn's car is gone. Only the Gardener's truck is there.

Gittes hurries along the pathway and up to the house. He rings the door
bell. Scarcely waiting for an answer, he tries it. It's locked. He reaches into

his pocket, pulls out his cigarette case, takes a pick out of the side, and starts to fool with the lock.

The Maid opens the door abruptly, stares in some surprise at Gittes.

> GITTES
>
> Where's Mrs. Mulwray?

> MAID
>
> No está.

215 Gittes looks past the Maid to the center of the living room—where luggage is packed and neatly piled.

The Maid is actually in the process of throwing covers over the furniture.

> GITTES
> *(indicating luggage)*
> Is Mrs. Mulwray going someplace? . . .
> *(no answer)*
> . . . on a trip? . . . Vacation? . . .

> MAID
>
> No está in casa.

Gittes nods. He continues through the house and out back to the veranda.

216 Ext. Mulwray Veranda—Gittes

is unsettled. Sees the Gardener working by the pond. He wanders a few yards in that direction.

217 Gardener

spots Gittes, half bows, nods, and smiles.

218 Gittes

in turn, nods, smiles.

> GITTES
>
> —bad for glass.

219 Gardener

breaks into a big grin. Nods again.

> GARDENER
>
> Oh, yes, bad for glass.

He points to the newly mown lawn.

> GARDENER
> *(continuing)*
>
> Salt water velly bad for glass.

220 Gittes

can't quite believe what he's heard.

> GITTES
>
> Salt water?

The Gardener nods vigorously. Points to the pond.

> GARDENER
>
> Velly, velly bad.

Gittes has moved to the pond. He kneels. Clinging to the edge of it, he can now see, as he could have before if he'd looked closely, a starfish.

221 Close Starfish

It has one leg missing. The fifth point on the star is just beginning to grow back.

222 Gittes

touches the water, tastes it. He licks his lips, then spots something glinting in the bottom of the pond.

> GITTES
>
> What's that . . . down there?

The Gardener peers into the pond.

> GITTES
> *(continuing)*
>
> *There.*

The Gardener spots it. He rolls up his trousers, gets in the pond, and reaches into the bottom, his chin actually touching the water. He misses the object, which seems to scoot away like an animal. Then he grasps it. He lifts it out of the water and holds a pair of eyeglasses, rimless, bent, his finger poking through the frame where one lens is shattered.

The Gardener seems surprised. Gittes looks at the glasses. They are heavily bifocal and reflect the sun.

223 Int. Mulwray Home

Gittes holds the phone to his ear. On the telephone table, lying on his handkerchief, are the glasses.

The Maid hovers around over Gittes' shoulder, watching him uneasily.

> CROSS' VOICE
>
> Hello.

> GITTES
>
> Have you got your checkbook handy, Mr. Cross? I've got the girl.

> CROSS' VOICE
>
> —you've got her? Where?

> GITTES
>
> Do you remember the figures we discussed?

> CROSS' VOICE
>
> Of course I do. Where are you?

> GITTES
>
> —at your daughter's house. How soon can you get here?

> CROSS' VOICE
>
> . . . Two hours. . . . Tell me, will Evelyn be there as well?

> GITTES
>
> Either that or she'll be in jail.

> CROSS' VOICE
>
> What are you talking about?

> GITTES
>
> Just bring your checkbook.

Gittes hangs up.

224 Ext. Bungalow-house, Adelaide Drive

Gittes pulls up in Mulwray's Buick. He hurries to the front door, pounds on it.

The Chinese Servant answers the door.

> CHINESE SERVANT
> You wait.

> GITTES
> *(short sentence in Chinese)*
> You wait.

225 Gittes pushes past him. Evelyn, looking a little worn but glad to see him, hurries to the door. She takes Gittes' arm.

> EVELYN
> How are you? I was calling you.

She looks at him, searching his face.

> GITTES
> —Yeah?

They move into the living room. Gittes is looking around it.

> EVELYN
> Did you get some sleep?

> GITTES
> Sure.

> EVELYN
> Did you have lunch? Kyo will fix you something—

> GITTES
> *(abruptly)*
> —where's the girl?

> EVELYN
> Upstairs. Why?

> GITTES
> I want to see her.

EVELYN

... she's having a bath now. . . . why do you want to
see her?

Gittes continues to look around. He sees clothes laid out for packing in a
bedroom off the living room.

GITTES

Going somewhere?

EVELYN

Yes, we've got a 4:30 train to catch. Why?

Gittes doesn't answer. He goes to the phone and dials.

GITTES

—J. J. Gittes for Lieutenant Escobar . . .

EVELYN

What are you doing? What's wrong? I told you
we've got a 4:30—

GITTES
(cutting her off)
You're going to miss your train!
(then, into phone)
. . . Lou, meet me at 1412 Adelaide Drive—it's above
Santa Monica Canyon. . . . yeah, soon as you can.

EVELYN

What did you do that for?

GITTES
(a moment, then)
You know any good criminal lawyers?

EVELYN
(puzzled)

—no . . .

GITTES

Don't worry—I can recommend a couple. They're
expensive, but you can afford it.

EVELYN
(evenly but with great anger)
What the hell is this all about?

Gittes looks at her, then takes the handkerchief out of his breast pocket, unfolds it on a coffee table, revealing the bifocal glasses, one lens still intact. Evelyn stares dumbly at them.

> GITTES
>
> I found these in your backyard—in your fish pond. They belonged to your husband, didn't they? . . . didn't they?

> EVELYN
>
> I don't know. I mean, yes, probably.

> GITTES
>
> —yes positively. That's where he was drowned. . . .

> EVELYN
>
> What are you saying?

> GITTES
>
> There's no time for you to be shocked by the truth, Mrs. Mulwray. The coroner's report proves he was killed in salt water. I want to know how it happened and why. I want to know before Escobar gets here. I want to hang on to my license.

> EVELYN
>
> I don't know what you're talking about. This is the most insane . . . the craziest thing I ever . . .

Gittes has been in a state of near frenzy himself. He gets up, shakes her.

> GITTES
>
> Stop it!—I'll make it easy—You were jealous, you fought, he fell, hit his head—it was an accident—but his girl is a witness. You've had to pay her off. You don't have the stomach to harm her, but you've got the money to shut her up. Yes or no?

> EVELYN
>
> . . . no . . .

> GITTES
>
> Who is she? And don't give me that crap about it
> being your sister. You don't have a sister.

Evelyn is trembling.

> EVELYN
>
> I'll tell you the truth. . . .

Gittes smiles.

> GITTES
>
> That's good. Now what's her name?

> EVELYN
>
> —Katherine.

> GITTES
>
> Katherine? . . . Katherine who?

> EVELYN
>
> —she's my daughter.

**226 Gittes stares at her. He's been charged with anger, and when Evelyn
says this, it explodes. He hits her full in the face. Evelyn stares back at
him. The blow has forced tears to her eyes, but she makes no move, not
even to defend herself.**

> GITTES
>
> I said the truth!

> EVELYN
>
> —she's my sister—

Gittes slaps her again.

> EVELYN
> (continuing)
>
> —she's my daughter.

Gittes slaps her again.

> EVELYN
> (continuing)
>
> —my sister.

He hits her again.

EVELYN
(continuing)
My daughter, my sister—

He belts her finally, knocking her into a cheap Chinese vase that shatters, and she collapses on the sofa, sobbing.

GITTES
I said I want the truth.

EVELYN
(almost screaming it)
She's my sister *and* my daughter!

Kyo comes running down the stairs.

EVELYN
(continuing)
For God's sake, Kyo, keep her upstairs. Go back!

Kyo turns after staring at Gittes for a moment, then goes back upstairs.

EVELYN
(continuing)
—my father and I, understand, or is it too tough for you?

Gittes doesn't answer.

EVELYN
(continuing)
. . . he had a breakdown . . . the dam broke . . . my mother died . . . he became a little boy . . . I was fifteen . . . he'd ask me what to eat for breakfast, what clothes to wear! It happened . . . then I ran away . . .

GITTES
. . . to Mexico . . .

She nods.

> EVELYN
>
> . . . Hollis came and took . . . care of me . . . after she
> was born . . . he said . . . he took care of her . . . I
> couldn't see her . . . I wanted to but I couldn't . . .
> I just want to see once in a while . . . take care
> of her . . . that's all . . . but I don't want her to
> know . . . I don't want her to know . . .

> GITTES
>
> . . . so that's why you hate him . . .

Evelyn slowly looks up at Gittes.

> EVELYN
>
> —no . . . for turning his back on me after it hap-
> pened! He couldn't face it . . .
> *(weeping)*
> I hate him.

Gittes suddenly feels the need to loosen his tie.

> GITTES
>
> —yeah . . . where are you taking her now?

> EVELYN
>
> Back to Mexico.

> GITTES
>
> You can't go by train. Escobar'll be looking for you
> everywhere.

> EVELYN
>
> How about a plane?

> GITTES
>
> That's worse . . . just get out of here—walk out,
> leave everything.

> EVELYN
>
> I have to go home and get my things—

> GITTES
>
> —I'll take care of it.

> EVELYN
>
> Where can we go?

GITTES

. . . where does Kyo live?

EVELYN

—with us.

GITTES

On his day off. Get the exact address.

EVELYN

—okay . . .

She stops suddenly.

EVELYN

Those didn't belong to Hollis.

For a moment Gittes doesn't know what she's talking about. Then he follows her gaze to the glasses lying on his handkerchief.

GITTES

How do you know?

EVELYN

He didn't wear bifocals.

Gittes picks up the glasses, stares at the lens, is momentarily lost in them.

227 Evelyn

from the stairs. She has her arm around Katherine.

EVELYN ·

Say hello to Mr. Gittes, sweetheart.

KATHERINE
(from the stairs)

Hello.

228 Gittes

rises a little shakily from the arm of the sofa.

GITTES

Hello.

With her arm around the girl, talking in Spanish, Evelyn hurries her toward the bedroom. In a moment she reemerges.

> EVELYN
> *(calling down)*
> —he lives at 1712 Alameda . . . do you know where
> that is?

229 Reaction—Gittes

He nods slowly.

> GITTES
> —sure. It's in Chinatown.

230 Thru Window

of bungalow Gittes watches Evelyn, the girl, and Kyo head for Kyo's black dusty sedan.

Gittes drops the curtain, heads swiftly to the phone. He dials.

> GITTES
> Sophie . . . is Walsh there? . . . yeah, listen, pal, Esco-
> bar's going to try and book me in about five min-
> utes. . . . relax, I'll tell you. Wait in the office for two
> hours. If you don't hear from me, you and Duffy
> meet me at 1712 Alameda.

> WALSH'S VOICE
> —Jesus, that's in Chinatown, ain't it?

231 The front BELL RINGS.

> GITTES
> I know where it is! Just do it.

Gittes hangs up and goes to the door. He opens it. No one is there.

> GITTES
> *(not even bothering to look around the sides)*
> Come on in, Lou—we're both too late.

Escobar and his minions appear from either side of the door.

> GITTES
> *(continuing)*
> Looks like she flew the coop.

Escobar nods.

ESCOBAR

I don't suppose you got any idea where she went?

GITTES

Matter of fact I do.

ESCOBAR

Where?

GITTES

Her maid's house. I think she knows something's
up.

ESCOBAR

What's the maid's address?

GITTES

She lives in Pedro—I'll write it down for you—

ESCOBAR

No, Gittes, you'll show us.

GITTES

What for?

ESCOBAR

If she's not there, you're going downtown, and
you're staying there til she shows up.

GITTES
(deliberately petulant)
Gee, Lou, I'm doing the best I can.

ESCOBAR
(shoving him toward the door)
Tell us about it on the way to Pedro.

232 Ext. San Pedro—29th Street—Day

A steep hill overlooking part of the harbor. Escobar's unmarked car pulls
up to a stop in front of a Spanish duplex perched on the steep hillside.

ESCOBAR

That's it?

GITTES

—yeah.

ESCOBAR

Well, let's go.

GITTES

Do me a favor, will you, Lou?

Escobar waits.

GITTES
(continuing)

Let me bring her down myself . . . she's not armed or
nothing . . . she won't be any problem . . . I'd just like
a minute alone with her . . . it would mean something . . . to . . . her . . . and to me.

Escobar shakes his head. For a moment it looks like it means no.

ESCOBAR

You never learn, do you, Gittes?

GITTES
(a little chagrined)

I guess not.

ESCOBAR

—Give you three minutes.

GITTES

Gee, thanks, Lou.

Gittes gets out of the car, glances around, goes up the stairs. He looks back
down at Escobar. Gittes rings the bell. He waits. It opens. It's a WOMAN
who's not recognizable. She's got the remnants of a black eye.

WOMAN

Yes? . . .

Gittes looks past her to Curly, the fisherman from the first scene. He's
seated at the dinner table with his father, his mother, and his children.
Curly looks up in surprise.

CURLY
(happily)

Mr. Gittes! Come in, come in.

233 Gittes enters and closes the door. Curly rises and comes over to him, greets him happily.

>   CURLY
> Gee, this is a surprise, Mr. Gittes.

>   GITTES
> Call me Jake. How is everything?

>   CURLY
> Just sitting down to supper, Jake. Care to join us?

>   GITTES
> No thanks.

>   CURLY
> How about a glass of wine? Honey, this is—

>   WIFE
>   *(coolly)*
> Yes, I know.

>   GITTES
> Thanks just the same, Curly. I could use a glass of
> water, tho—come out with me to the kitchen for a
> second.

>   CURLY
>   *(puzzled)*
> Sure thing.

234 Int. Kitchen—Gittes and Curly

>   GITTES
> Curly, where's your car?

>   CURLY
> In the garage.

>   GITTES
> Where's that?

>   CURLY
> Off the alley.

                            GITTES
—Could you drive me somewhere?

                            CURLY
Sure, as soon as we eat—

                            GITTES
Right now, Curly. It can't wait.

                            CURLY
I'll just tell my wife.

                            GITTES
                    (pulling him out the back door)
—tell her later.

They head out the back door and down the steps toward the garage.

235 Ext. Alley and Garage

Curly pulls open the garage door. Gets in, starts the car, backs it out. It's an old, late twenties Plymouth sedan. Gittes hops in. They take off. At the edge of the alley, Gittes looks back.

235A POV from Curly's Car

Escobar is getting out of his car, moving toward the duplex. Gittes slips down in the seat.

                        GITTES' VOICE
Just drive slow for a block or two, will you, Curly?

                        CURLY'S VOICE
What's this all about?

                        GITTES' VOICE
Tell you in a couple of blocks.

236 Int. Sedan—Gittes and Curly

                            GITTES
How much do you owe me, Curly?

CURLY
(embarrassed)

Oh, gee, Mr. Gittes—we're going out tomorrow. I know you been real good about it, but my cousin Auggie's sick.

GITTES

Forget it. How would you like to pay me off by taking a couple of passengers to Ensenada . . . you'd have to leave tonight.

CURLY

—I don't know . . .

GITTES

—I might be able to squeeze an extra seventy-five bucks out of it for you—maybe an even hundred.

CURLY

—plus what I owe you?

GITTES

I'll throw that in too.

CURLY
(smiling)
Okay, you got yourself a boat.

237 Ext. Mulwray Home—Gittes and Curly

carry bags out to Curly's car. Curly opens the door for the Maid. She gets in. He turns to Gittes.

GITTES

Tell Mrs. Mulwray to wait for half an hour after you get there—then if I don't show, take her down to the boat.

CURLY
(a little worried)
—you sure this is okay?

> GITTES
> *(mildly indignant)*
> Curly, you know how long I been in business?

Curly nods, reassured. He gets in and takes off.

238 Ext. Mulwray Home—Dusk

by the pond. Cigarette smoke drifts INTO SHOT. A car pulls up. In a moment Cross can be SEEN, looking TOWARD CAMERA.

> CROSS
> There you are.

He walks toward Gittes, who stands by the pond, smoking.

> CROSS
> *(continuing)*
> Well, you don't look any the worse for wear, Mr.
> Gittes, I must say. . . . where's the girl?

> GITTES
> I've got her.

> CROSS
> Is she all right?

> GITTES
> She's fine.

> CROSS
> Where is she?

> GITTES
> With her mother.

Cross' tone alters here.

> CROSS
> . . . with her mother?

Gittes pulls something out of his pocket and unfolds it.

> GITTES
> I'd like you to look at something, Mr. Cross—

                    CROSS
                  (taking it)
What is it?

                    GITTES
An obituary column . . . can you read in this light?

                    CROSS
Yes . . . I think I can manage. . . .

Cross dips into his coat pocket and pulls out a pair of rimless glasses. He
puts them on, reads.

239 Gittes

stares at the bifocal lenses as Cross continues to look through the obituary
column. He looks up.

                    CROSS
What does this mean?

                    GITTES
—that you killed Hollis Mulwray—

Gittes is holding the bifocals with the broken lens now.

                    GITTES
                  (continuing)
—right here, in this pond. You drowned him . . . and
you left these.

Cross looks at the glasses.

                    GITTES
. . . the coroner's report showed Mulwray had salt
water in his lungs.

                    CROSS
                  (finally)
Hollie was always fond of tide pools. You know
what he used to say about them?

                    GITTES
Haven't the faintest idea.

CROSS

—that's where life begins . . . marshes, sloughs, tide
pools . . . he was fascinated by them. . . . you know
when we first came out here, he figured that if you
dumped water onto desert sand, it would percolate
down into the bedrock and stay there, instead of
evaporating the way it does in most reservoirs.
You'd lose only twenty percent stead of seventy or
eighty. He made this city.

GITTES

—and that's what you were going to do in the Valley?

240 Ext. Pond—Cross and Mulwray

CROSS

(after a long moment)

—no, Mr. Gittes. That's what I *am* doing with the
Valley. The bond issue passes Tuesday—there'll be
ten million to build an aqueduct and reservoir. I'm
doing it.

GITTES

There's going to be some irate citizens when they
find out they're paying for water they're not getting.

CROSS

That's all taken care of. You see, Mr. Gittes. Either
you bring the water to L.A.—or you bring L.A. to
the water.

GITTES

How do you do that?

CROSS

—just incorporate the Valley into the city so the
water goes to L.A. after all. It's very simple.

Gittes nods.

GITTES

(then)

How much are you worth?

                    CROSS
                (shrugs, then)
I have no idea. How much do you want?

                    GITTES
I want to know what you're worth—over ten million?

                    CROSS
Oh, my, yes.

                    GITTES
Then why are you doing it? How much better can
you eat? What can you buy that you can't already
afford?

                    CROSS
            (a long moment, then:)
The future, Mr. Gittes—the future. Now where's the
girl? . . . I want the only daughter I have left . . . as
you found out, Evelyn was lost to me a long time
ago.

                    GITTES
                (with sarcasm)
Who do you blame for that? Her?

Cross makes a funny little cock of his head.

                    CROSS
I don't blame myself. You see, Mr. Gittes, most people never have to face the fact that at the right time
and right place, they're capable of anything. Take
those glasses from him, will you, Claude?

Mulvihill hoves INTO View. Extends his hand for the glasses. Gittes
doesn't move.

                    CROSS
                (continuing)
—it's not worth it, Mr. Gittes. It's really not worth it.

Gittes hands over the glasses.

> CROSS
> *(continuing)*
> Take us to the girl. Either Evelyn allows me to see
> her, or I'm not averse to seeing Evelyn in jail—if I
> have to buy the jail. Hollis and Evelyn kept her from
> me for fifteen years—it's been too long, I'm too old.

241 Ext. Chinatown Street—Night

The streets are crowded. Here and there one can see Chinese in traditional dress.

242 Gittes

driving slowly—spots Katherine with Ramon and luggage, nearly lost in the crowd. They are walking toward a car parked near a laundry truck.

Gittes sees them, keeps driving.

> CROSS
> *(suddenly)*
> Stop the car. Stop the car!

Mulvihill tries to clobber Gittes. Gittes elbows him. The car jumps the curb and hits a lamppost.

243 Ext. Street—Cross

leaps out of the car, shouting.

> CROSS
> Katherine! Katherine! Wait!

Gittes is after him, grabbing him. Cross tries to swing at Gittes with his cane. Mulvihill comes up behind Gittes, and the three of them begin an awkward wrestling match, the crowd scattering, Mulvihill pulling his revolver, trying to hit Gittes on the side of the head. The three men crash to the pavement.

244 Curly

starts out of the car toward Gittes. Gittes sees him.

> GITTES
> No, Curly, get 'em out of here! Get 'em out of here!

He bites Mulvihill's hand and furiously pounds it into the sidewalk, shaking the gun loose. Mulvihill and Gittes try for it, but someone else has it.

245 Evelyn

holds the gun. She's shaking but apparently in control of herself.

246 Gittes

rises to his feet. Mulvihill starts to help Cross up.

>   EVELYN
> No, don't help him. Don't do anything.

Mulvihill doesn't move. Cross rises on his own. Evelyn holds the revolver on him.

>   EVELYN
>   *(continuing)*
> She's gone. It's no good.

>   CROSS
> Where?

>   GITTES
>   *(moving to Evelyn)*
> Let me handle that.

>   EVELYN
>   *(to Gittes)*
> I'm all right.

>   GITTES
>   *(she's not)*
> Sure, but I'd like to handle it.

Evelyn backs up as her father takes a step toward her.

>   CROSS
> You're going to have to kill me, Evelyn. Either that
> or tell me where she is.

Evelyn is backing up. Cross moving on her. Evelyn cocks the pistol.

CROSS
(continuing)
How many years have I got? . . . she's mine too.

EVELYN
—she's never going to know that.

There's the SOUND of a SIREN. Cross lunges toward her. Gittes grabs Cross.

Duffy and Walsh are elbowing through the crowd. Gittes sees them.

GITTES
Duffy—go over and sit on Mulvihill.
(to Walsh)
Jesus Christ, I didn't tell you to bring the police department with you.

WALSH
Jake—it's Chinatown. They're all over the place. You oughta know better.

GITTES
(to Walsh, meaning Cross)
Gimme your keys. Watch this old fart, will you?
(moving to Evelyn)
Take Duffy's car. Curly's boat's in Pedro, near the Starkist cannery. It's the *Evening Star*. He'll be waiting. I'll take care of this.

247 She looks to Gittes. He looks at her. She turns and moves toward the car. Escobar is standing between her and it.

ESCOBAR
Mrs. Mulwray, you don't want to run around like that.

GITTES
Oh, Christ. Escobar, you don't know what's going on. Let her go. I'll explain it later.

ESCOBAR
Mrs. Mulwray, it's a very serious offense—pointing that at an officer of the law. It's a felony.

GITTES

Let her go. She didn't kill anybody.

ESCOBAR
(starting toward her)
I'm sorry, Mrs. Mulwray—

GITTES

Lou, she will kill you—let her go for now. You don't know.

ESCOBAR

Gittes, stay outta this.

Escobar continues to move toward her. Gittes grabs him.

GITTES
(to Evelyn)
Now take off.

Evelyn gets in the car. She starts it. Gittes lets Escobar go.

ESCOBAR

I'll just have her followed—she's not going anywhere—

There's a single GUNSHOT. Both men look surprised. Down the block, a uniformed officer has fired, standing beside his double-parked car. Duffy's sedan slows to a stop in the middle of the street. It jerks a couple of times, still in gear, then comes to a halt.

Gittes rushes to the car. He opens it. Evelyn falls out, inert. Blood is pouring from her right eye.

GITTES
(yelling)
No!

He holds on to Evelyn as Escobar and the others hurry up. Cross, himself, elbows through.

GITTES
(continuing)
Where is he? I'll kill him, I'll kill the son of a bitch—

Several officers contain Gittes.

> GITTES
> *(continuing, to Escobar)*
> Who is he, get his name? I'll kill him—

> ESCOBAR
> *(badly shaken)*
> Take it easy, take it easy, it was an accident—

> GITTES

An accident—

Gittes looks down. What he sees horrifies him. Cross is on the ground, holding Evelyn's body, crying.

> GITTES
> Get him away from her. He's responsible for everything. Get him away from her!

> ESCOBAR
> *(stunned)*
> Jake—you're very disturbed. You're crazy. That's her father.

Walsh and Duffy elbow through the crowd.

> ESCOBAR
> *(continuing, to them)*
> You wanna do your partner the biggest favor of his life? Take him home. Just get him the hell out of here!

Duffy bear-hugs the protesting Gittes, along with Walsh, literally dragging him away from the scene, with Gittes trying to shake free. Through the crowd noises, Walsh can be heard saying, "Forget it, Jake—it's Chinatown."

THE END